The Christmas Kiss

Hardman Holidays Book 10
A Sweet Historical Holiday Western Romance
by
USA TODAY Bestselling Author
SHANNA HATFIELD

Wholesome Hearts
PUBLISHING

The Christmas Kiss
Hardman Holidays Book 10

Copyright ©2022 by Shanna Hatfield

ISBN: 9798366841412

This is a work of fiction. Names, characters, businesses, places, events, and incidents either are the product of the author's imagination or are used in a fictitious manner. Any resemblance to actual persons, living or dead, business establishments, or actual events is purely coincidental.

Cover Design: Covers & Cupcakes

Published by Wholesome Hearts Publishing, LLC.
wholesomeheartspublishing@gmail.com

To the resilient…

Books by Shanna Hatfield

FICTION

CONTEMPORARY

Holiday Brides
Valentine Bride
Summer Bride
Easter Bride
Lilac Bride
Lake Bride

Rodeo Romance
The Christmas Cowboy
Wrestling Christmas
Capturing Christmas
Barreling Through Christmas
Chasing Christmas
Racing Christmas
Keeping Christmas
Roping Christmas
Remembering Christmas
Savoring Christmas

Grass Valley Cowboys
The Cowboy's Christmas Plan
The Cowboy's Spring Romance
The Cowboy's Summer Love
The Cowboy's Autumn Fall
The Cowboy's New Heart
The Cowboy's Last Goodbye

Summer Creek
Catching the Cowboy
Rescuing the Rancher
Protecting the Princess
Distracting the Deputy
Guiding the Grouch

Women of Tenacity
Heart of Clay
Heart of Hope
Heart of Love

HISTORICAL

Pendleton Petticoats
Dacey   *Bertie*
Aundy   *Millie*
Caterina   *Dally*
Ilsa   *Quinn*
Marnie   *Evie*
Lacey   *Sadie*

Baker City Brides
Crumpets and Cowpies
Thimbles and Thistles
Corsets and Cuffs
Bobbins and Boots
Lightning and Lawmen
Dumplings and Dynamite

Hearts of the War
Garden of Her Heart
Home of Her Heart
Dream of Her Heart

Hardman Holidays
The Christmas Bargain
The Christmas Token
The Christmas Calamity
The Christmas Vow
The Christmas Quandary
The Christmas Confection
The Christmas Melody
The Christmas Ring
The Christmas Wish
The Christmas Kiss

Holiday Express
Holiday Hope
Holiday Heart
Holiday Home
Holiday Love

Chapter One

1909

"Whoa, boys! Whoa up there!" the driver called as the stagecoach rolled to a stop amid swirls of dust and jangling harnesses that sounded like discordant Christmas bells.

Gracy Randall glanced out the window. *Home.* She was finally home. Almost six years had passed since the last time she'd been at Juniper Creek Ranch, a place that had been in her family since her grandparents had started it more than sixty years ago.

The ranch looked the same, with cattle in the pastures and harvested wheat fields, and yet so different. Her parents hadn't mentioned putting up a new ranch sign, but it looked nice, as did the fresh coat of paint on the house, barn, and outbuildings.

The letter she'd received last week hadn't included any reference to the vast array of improvements. If the newly set towering poles marching up the lane like wooden sentinels were any indication, her parents had recently had a telephone installed.

Gracy could hardly set her mind to accept all the changes that had taken place. Perhaps her parents had kept it all a secret in hopes of letting her be amazed when she finally returned to the small Eastern Oregon community of Hardman.

If that was the case, she supposed they'd be equally surprised she'd returned. Although they'd been planning to make the trip to Grass Valley, where Gracy had lived and worked since leaving Hardman, she was ready to come back home. Not just for a visit but permanently.

Excited about returning, she'd been eagerly anticipating the expressions on her parents' faces when she walked into the kitchen and greeted them.

Since the ranch was on the stage route into Hardman, she'd asked the driver to let her off there. The trunks with her belongings would arrive tomorrow on a freight wagon. For now, everything she needed was in one travel bag she could easily carry the short distance from the road to the home where she'd grown up.

With one more glance out the window, Gracy moved toward the door with as much poise as possible in the crowded stagecoach. She'd ridden all the way from Heppner crammed between two roughly attired men who'd both sprawled out their legs the moment they'd taken seats on either side of her.

"Pardon me," she said, trying to step around the one closest to the door. The man offered her a lecherous grin and started to reach a hand toward her backside. Before he had a chance, she swatted him with her beaded reticule, causing the rest of the occupants of the stagecoach to laugh.

Gracy glowered at her fellow passengers as she pushed open the door and grabbed onto the frame to balance herself. It seemed not a single gentleman had ridden on the conveyance from Heppner.

"You sure you want off here?" the driver asked from his perch at the front of the stagecoach as she tried to keep her balance, discreetly hold her skirts out of her way, and heft her traveling bag.

"Absolutely certain," she said, growing more riled by the second. One of the horses angrily switched his tail at a horsefly and took a step forward, causing the stagecoach to rock and throw her off balance.

A rough, calloused hand appeared in front of her face, but instead of accepting the belatedly offered assistance, she hopped off the steps and landed with an "umph" on both feet. Dust rose in a cloud and coated her already filthy traveling suit she doubted would ever come clean.

She knew it had been a dry year in the area from her mother's letters, but she'd had no idea how dry until the dust had fogged into the stagecoach with every passing mile. She'd expected it to be cold, but even in mid-November, the weather was mild and warm, feeling more like a spring day.

Gracy adjusted the hat that had slid over one eye back into a fashionable angle, drew in a deep breath, straightened her spine, and started down the lane toward the house.

"She's as fiery as her hair," she heard one of the men comment before the driver snapped the lines and set the stagecoach into motion again.

Gracy had never been fond of her red hair and, in fact, had no idea from whom she'd inherited it. Both of her parents had brown hair, and so had her brother Rob. Her mother had assured her it was from a great-grandmother who'd arrived in America from Ireland nearly a century earlier, but it did nothing to help her feel better about the ginger hue of her locks.

As she walked up the lane, she thought of Percy Bruner, a boy she'd known all her life. His parents had owned the mercantile in town for as long as Gracy could recall. Percy had the brightest, reddest hair she'd ever seen. He'd left Hardman not long before Gracy had packed her things and moved to Grass Valley, but he'd returned and was now a well-known photographer in the region.

Unwilling to think of the reasons so many people had left—the reasons she'd left—she released a long breath and continued toward the house. Two dogs she didn't recognize ran out of the barn, barking at her arrival. Her parents hadn't mentioned getting any new canines. She wondered where old Bentley was hiding. He'd been a puppy when her parents had given the dog to her for

Christmas when she was sixteen. She'd had such fun training him and teaching him tricks, but he was nine, so he likely wasn't as spry as he once was.

The two dogs circled around her, tails wagging. Gracy tucked her reticule inside her traveling bag, then set the leather satchel on the ground, leaving two hands free for petting the dogs. They sniffed her gloved fingers and whined, so she rubbed them along their backs and scratched behind their ears. She could see what looked like a bit of collie in the mutts mixed with goodness only knew what. Regardless of their pedigree, the dogs were good-natured and friendly, two important characteristics in her opinion.

"That's all for now," Gracy said, wiping her gloves on her skirt before picking up her bag.

The dogs woofed and ran back toward the barn just as Gracy heard a loud thwacking sound. Curious about the source creating the noise, she hastened her steps and was nearly to the house when she noticed a child wearing dusty overalls. The boy couldn't have been more than six or seven, making her wonder why he wasn't in school instead of destroying ranch property.

The little menace swung a mallet, mercilessly beating the wooden hitching rail her father had installed just outside of the yard's fence when Gracy had been eight. She'd helped her father set the two posts, then add the crosspiece. Now, an unruly monster was about to beat it into splinters with a mallet she was sure had once belonged to her grandfather.

"What on earth are you doing?" she asked as she rushed up to the child. He had a mop of dark brown hair, brown eyes snapping with liveliness and a determined look on his impish face. If he hadn't been possessed with pure mischief, she may have even thought him adorable.

As it was, he ignored her and continued to pound the rail with randomly placed swings.

Gracy looked around, but there was no visiting buggy or automobile parked anywhere she could see. Her mother hadn't mentioned any children coming to visit or to stay. Heaven forbid the future degenerate refusing to speak to her had been left with her parents. They were far too old to keep up with a youngster like him. They'd been in their forties when she'd been born. The last thing they needed was a puckish youngster running amok on the ranch.

"Where is your mother?" Gracy raised her voice to be heard over the boy's pounding.

The mallet stopped mid-swing and the child raised his gaze to hers. Rather than answer, his eyes welled with tears, then he returned to whacking the rail with renewed force.

Gracy thought about wresting the mallet away from him, but she feared being struck with it. "You need to stop that. You'll turn it into a pile of splinters at the rate you're going."

The boy acted as though he hadn't heard a word she'd said. What kind of misbehaving riffraff had moved to Hardman? Surely, she would have recalled her mother mentioning any new families with young children visiting the ranch.

"Cease your hammering!" Gracy yelled to be heard above the pounding.

He gave her a dismissive glare, moved beyond her reach, and continued to whack the rail.

Annoyed with the little hooligan, Gracy marched through the gate, across the stepping stones she'd helped her father set in the lawn ten years ago, and raced up the porch steps. The rocking chairs her parents used to sit on of an evening had disappeared. Had her mother finally decided to replace them, or had the boy destroyed them, beating the chairs into a pile of kindling?

Distraught, Gracy turned the knob on the door and sailed into the house. She was halfway across the entry area before she slid to a stop, gawking around with her mouth hanging open in shock.

The entry was no longer painted the sickly hue of mauve she'd long detested but a warm, buttery shade of yellow. A new oak floor gleamed from a recent polish, and new paned windows allowed sunlight to spill inside. How had she not noticed the windows earlier? Then again, she'd been so distracted by the miniature demon with the mallet, she had likely overlooked many details.

"Mama?" she called as she set her bag on the floor and stepped into the parlor. Gone was the dark plum wallpaper and the walnut furniture that was familiar. The walls had been covered in expensive embossed cream paper with tiny blue flowers and feathery vines. Three leather wingback chairs, one of them a rocker, were spread out around a long dark blue camelback sofa that looked comfortable and inviting. The end tables and lamps all appeared new. If she hadn't been so taken aback by the changes, she would have found the room quite fetching.

She sucked in a gasp when she realized her grandmother's piano was no longer there. Gracy had loved playing it, especially during the holidays. Her grandmother had taught Gracy to play when she'd been no bigger than the child still loudly wreaking havoc outside.

"Mama!" The volume of Gracy's voice increased along with her confusion. She stepped into the dining room to find all new furnishings there. The cream wallpaper covering the walls featured pale yellow roses and sage-colored leaves nestled in vertical rows between stripes of light blue. A large mahogany china cupboard held an expensive set of china decorated with bright blue flowers and scrolls.

"What has happened?" Gracy muttered to herself, wondering if her parents had come into a windfall of money. She couldn't begin to imagine from where it would originate, though. Her grandparents, all four of them, had passed away years ago. There were no wealthy aunts or uncles. How could her parents afford to not just redecorate the house, but to decorate it with such costly furnishings and goods?

Gracy walked into the kitchen. The room bore a fresh coat of white paint and new black and white tiles on the floor. The old walnut cabinets had been removed and new white cabinets, several with glass fronts, took their place. New windows, in need of a good wash, had been installed over a deep sink.

Beginning to feel lightheaded, Gracy turned to go out the back door, only to realize the doorway now opened into a hallway instead of outside. She stood on wobbly legs, contemplating if she'd tumbled down a magical rabbit hole that had deposited her somewhere other than the home where she'd grown up.

Grown up. That was it! She backtracked to the entry and charged up the stairs. Everywhere she looked, she saw changes in the paint, wallpaper, flooring, and furnishings. Perhaps she had gotten off at the wrong place, but the Juniper Creek Ranch sign had been out front, and it was the only ranch by that name in the whole county.

She half-jogged down the hall to the room that had been hers and ran her fingers over the doorframe where her father had marked her growth each year. The numbers were still there, along with her father's notation of her age. She wasn't crazy. It was her childhood home. But where were her parents? How could they have changed everything about the house without even mentioning it to her?

Her bedroom looked nothing like she recalled the last time she'd been in the room. Instead of her washstand, chest of drawers, and simple iron bed, a beautifully carved golden oak bedroom set filled the room. Gone was the quilt her grandmother had made for her. A coverlet with embroidered yellow and blue flowers now spread over the bed.

"Mama! Papa!" she hollered, growing more disturbed by the second.

No one answered her, so she rushed back down the stairs and into the kitchen, then stepped into the new hallway. At the far end of it, she found an exterior door and walked onto a back porch that had been added.

Outside, she dragged in a deep breath, trying to fathom what had taken place at the ranch. At least the big juniper tree that had stood between the house and barn her entire life was still there.

Gracy marched down the porch steps and returned out front, where she tossed a withering glare at the boy who had moved from the hitching rail to smacking the mallet against the stepping stones in the yard. If he were any bigger or stronger, there was a chance he'd split them in two.

Distressed and fuming, Gracy rushed toward the barn. She thought it odd none of the hired hands had noticed her arrival. Tug Tallman had been there for thirty years as the foreman and had always been like a second father to her.

"Mama? Papa?" she called as she sped into the barn. "Tug?"

Even the inside of the barn looked different, although she couldn't say exactly why. Then she saw four horses she didn't recognize in the stalls. "What is this?"

"What's what?" a deep masculine voice asked from behind her, scaring her so badly she screamed and jumped a foot off the ground.

Uncertain who might be sneaking up on her, she snatched the long pin securing her hat from her hair and held it in front of her like a weapon as she turned to face the unwelcome intruder.

She hadn't anticipated he'd be quite so young or good-looking with his heavily lashed hazel eyes, square chin, and snub nose. Tall, broad-shouldered, and muscular, he appeared to be a man who worked hard for a living.

He was dressed in worn denims with a blue flannel shirt, a dusty cowboy hat, and scuffed cowboy boots. From the chaps and spurs he wore, she assumed he'd been out riding. Something about him seemed familiar, but she had no idea as to what or why.

Involuntarily, she breathed in a whiff of his scent, one that smelled of horses and sunshine, and all man.

Annoyed with herself, with the child bent on demolition, and the cowboy grinning at her with a wide, easy smile that made the most charming lines pop out around his eyes and in the creases of his cheeks, she huffed in frustration. "I'm looking for Everett and Cleo Randall. Are they gone for the day?"

The cowboy removed his hat, ran a hand through his thick medium brown hair, and offered her a studying glance. Something in the way he looked at her, like he could peer into her soul and see every secret hidden in her heart, left her flustered and peevish. She could feel heat creeping up her neck and stinging her cheeks under his perusal. By sheer determination, she willed herself to remain calm even though she felt like stamping her feet and demanding the whereabouts of her parents.

"Where are Mr. and Mrs. Randall?" she asked in a tight voice.

The man shrugged. "I reckon they're ..."

A loud crack from the direction of the yard drew her out of the barn in time to see the child holding up a broken piece of stepping stone. Apparently, he was far stronger than she'd assumed to break one of the stones into pieces.

"That is the most ill-behaved child I've ever encountered. Do you know to whom he belongs? He's nearly beaten the hitching post to death despite my instruction to leave it alone. Now he's focused on obliterating the walk. His parents should take matters in hand and discipline the miscreant."

The man's smile disappeared in an instant, replaced with a harsh glower. "As a matter of fact, he's my son. Bodie's not hurting a thing. I'm planning to put in a new walk anyway." He took a menacing step toward her, and she could feel the anger rolling off him like a palpable force. "You have no right to march in here and say anything to my son. You don't know him, or anything about him, missy, so I'll thank you to mind your tongue and your own business."

"I have every right to be here. This is my home." About to lose the tenuous hold she had on her rising temper, Gracy pinned the stranger with a frosty glare. "Who are you?"

The man returned the hat to his head, took a step back from her, and widened his stance. "Cord Granger. As of eight months ago, I took over as the owner of Juniper Creek Ranch."

Gracy felt woozy. For a moment, she thought she might faint for the first time in her life.

How could her parents sell their home and not even mention it to her? If she hadn't returned to town, would they ever have told her? And where were they? She'd still been sending letters to them at the post office in Hardman. Had they moved to a different town?

Mr. Granger sneered at her. "I'm gonna guess you're Everett and Cleo's daughter. I can see a resemblance to your mother, although she's a much kinder and far less judgmental person. Frankly, after hearing your parents sing your praises, I expected ... well, not you."

Indignant, Gracy felt like she'd been handed a great insult, even if it had only been implied. Adamant that Mr. Granger not see any weakness in her, she forced herself to focus on one problem at a time.

"Where are my parents?"

"Hardman, as far as I know. They built a new house across the street from the Bruner family."

Gracy frowned. "George and Aleta no longer live above the mercantile?"

Cord shook his head. "They're still there. Percy Bruner and his wife bought Tia and Adam Guthry's house."

Gracy recalled her mother mentioning something about Percy having married Brynn Rutherford after he'd returned to Hardman last year. She'd forgotten that detail. If Percy could not only come back to a town he'd vowed to never set foot in again but also find happiness and love, maybe there was still hope for her.

Another loud crack drew Gracy's attention back to the front yard. The boy grinned as he gleefully swung the mallet with frenzied, reckless movements. Mr. Granger would be fortunate if the child didn't break a window before the afternoon was through.

"Isn't he old enough to behave better than that? Perhaps if he weren't being raised by a cavedweller he'd have better manners," she said, unable to stop herself from speaking her mind. "At his age, why isn't he in school? You're fortunate a truant officer hasn't been to pay a call."

"He's not yet five, and he isn't doing anything wrong. It's been unseasonably warm the past few days. A bunch of flies came out of hiding, and Bodie takes great pleasure in smacking them with the mallet that your father gave to him. As I already stated, he's not hurting anything, so leave him alone." The scowl he turned on her looked both intimidating and frightening. "Since the odds are high that you're going to say something else I'm likely to take offense to, I'd appreciate it if you'd take your high and mighty attitude and haul it off my property, Miss Randall."

Before she could utter a word of protest, the cowboy grabbed her arm and pulled her toward the lane. Still armed with her hatpin, she briefly considered burying it into his hand, but instead, poked it back into her hat.

"Unhand me!" She jerked away from him with such force, she had to take three quick steps to keep from tripping over her twisted skirt.

The look of amusement on Mr. Granger's face only served to stoke the fire of her fury.

Regardless of how childish it was, she stamped both feet. "I do not find anything humorous about any of this, Mr. Granger! Not a thing!"

"I don't rightly find much to laugh about in this situation either, Miss Randall. Now go. Until you can talk without screeching and treat my son with kindness, don't come back."

"Fine!" Gracy fisted her skirt in her hands, lifting it up a few inches so she could walk unimpeded.

Rage fueled her steps as she strode to the road, then turned toward Hardman. She was a mile closer to town when she realized she'd left her bag sitting in the entry of the house. She'd rather crawl through a pit filled with riled rattlesnakes than return to *that* man's house. He'd made it abundantly clear she wasn't welcome.

If she never again set eyes on Cord Granger, it would be just fine with her. Only the likelihood of that happening was close to impossible since he was no doubt related to the Grangers who lived in Hardman and had been pillars of the community for years.

Now that she thought about it, Cord did bear a resemblance to Luke Granger. She wondered if they were cousins, since she knew Luke and his sister Ginny had no other siblings. Not that she cared.

It would please her greatly if Cord Granger packed up and left before she had to encounter him again. The man was positively detestable.

Chapter Two

Cord Granger tipped back his hat with the tip of his thumb, wiped the sweat beading on his forehead on his shirtsleeve, and watched the red-headed tyrant known as Gracy Randall storm down his lane. Her skirts swished around her slender ankles with every angry step, kicking up a cloud of dust in her wake.

How the feisty, fiery, flame-haired, fractious, fascinating female could be related to Everett and Cleo Randall boggled his mind. If it hadn't been for her resemblance to Cleo, he would never have thought to connect her to the kindhearted, caring couple who'd become like family to him.

After losing his wife, and then his parents, Cord had felt driven to get away from the sadness that had lingered in his home in Boston. His career in investment banking had seemed so meaningless after Helen's death.

Cord had recalled some of the happiest times in his life had been spent on a ranch in Texas owned by his mother's uncle. Of course, the uncle was gone now, and Cord held no interest in moving to Texas, but he'd known he had to leave Boston.

His cousins, Lila Granger Grove as well as siblings Luke and Ginny Granger, had all settled in a little town in Eastern Oregon. Even his discerning Aunt Dora lived there, mostly to be close to her children and grandchildren. But if it was good enough for her, Cord had been sure he'd like it.

Back in February, he'd written to Luke and asked about any properties for sale. Luke had replied immediately, and before Cord had quite known what had happened, he'd purchased Juniper Creek Ranch. He hadn't cared if the house was in shambles and the buildings were on the verge of collapse. All he'd known at the time was that buying a place in Hardman would give him an opportunity for the fresh start he and Bodie so badly needed.

A month later, he and Bodie had arrived in Hardman in a newly purchased wagon he'd ordered and had shipped, along with a fine team of horses to pull it, to Heppner, the closest town with a railroad. Upon arriving, Cord and Bodie had gone straight to Granger House, where Luke and his family had welcomed them. After Luke's wife, Filly, had spoiled them with a delicious meal and Bodie had gotten a chance to play with his cousins, Cord had signed the papers and paid Everett and Cleo Randall, making Juniper Creek Ranch his.

When he found out Mr. and Mrs. Randall had purchased a lot in town but construction on the house was not yet complete, he'd invited them to stay at the ranch while their home was built. Cleo's help with the house and Bodie had been invaluable, while Everett had taught Cord all he needed to know about the ranch and made a smooth transition for him with the ranch hands.

In the process, Cord felt like he'd not only gained friends in the elderly couple but also found someone to fill the role of grandparents to Bodie.

Not once in all the months he'd been there had he regretted his decision to leave Boston for Oregon. The first few months they'd been in Hardman, he'd enlisted the help of Filly and Ginny to redecorate the house. They'd been able to choose colors, styles, and patterns that not only were ones he liked but also made the house feel like home.

Cleo hadn't seemed to mind in the least as he'd changed each room to make it his own. She'd confided in him that Everett's grandmother had originally decorated the house and most of what the woman had chosen was not to her liking. Cleo had never said a word to her husband about it because it was his family home and he had so many memories tied to it.

Cord thought it had been much harder for Everett to leave the ranch than it had been for Cleo. Still, the old rancher found plenty of reasons to stop by when he wasn't working at the newspaper office in town or drinking coffee with some of the other old-timers. Not that Everett was all that old. Seventy wasn't exactly ancient, and Everett could still run circles around most of the ranch hands. Cord hoped he'd be as spry as Everett when he reached that age.

Although he'd known the couple had a daughter, it wasn't until he'd set eyes on her that the truth of Gracy's age, close to his own, had hit him. For some reason, he'd always envisioned her as older and bookish.

He knew Gracy had left Hardman, like so many others, after a wicked influenza had swept through town and claimed many lives, including that of her fiancé and the Randalls' son, Rob, along with his young family. From what Cord understood, Gracy hadn't set foot back in Hardman since she'd moved to Grass Valley almost six years ago, and had no plans to ever return.

The couple had gone to visit Gracy in May, but they'd never made mention of what she thought about their selling the ranch.

Now, he wished they'd gotten around to sharing the news with her so he wouldn't have borne the brunt of her displeasure at what was clearly unwelcome news.

Earlier, he'd thought he'd heard a woman's voice while he'd been working with a colt in the corral behind the barn. He'd left the colt tied to the fence and stepped into the barn to find a woman standing there, appearing perplexed. For a moment, he'd been entirely dumbfounded by her beauty.

SHANNA HATFIELD

Gracy Randall had hair the color of a cozy winter fire, warm blue eyes, and creamy, flawless skin. Her high cheekbones, pink lips, and cute nose that turned up just slightly on the tip had made him give her a longer study. She'd worn a dust-coated gray jacket and skirt, and her hat had looked like it might never come clean, but she truly was lovely.

Then he'd spoken and startled her. She'd spun around to face him, a long hatpin clenched in her fist like a weapon. The notion of her trying to fend off someone with a hatpin had made him want to laugh, but he'd hidden his mirth beneath a welcoming smile.

In a blink, the situation rapidly tumbled downhill. Cord had taken exception when she'd lambasted Bodie and called him names. Admittedly, he'd probably said a few things he shouldn't have.

On the verge of losing his temper, Cord had grabbed her arm and headed toward the lane, eager to have her off the place. She'd held the hatpin in her fist and glanced at him like she considered impaling it into some part of his anatomy. Much to his relief, she'd jammed it back into her hat before she succumbed to the urge, then jerked away from him with such force she'd nearly tripped over her tangled skirt.

Amused by her mistaken idea she was a force to be reckoned with, Cord couldn't help but smirk at her, further invoking her wrath. When she'd stamped her feet like a toddler in the throes of a tantrum, he'd briefly considered threatening to paddle her backside if she continued to act like a spoiled child, but had thought better of it. As angry

24

as she'd been, she might have yanked out that hatpin again and plunged it somewhere it could have done real damage.

Frustrated, incensed, and insulted by her harsh words, Cord was further peeved he couldn't seem to look away as he stood rooted to the spot, watching each furious step she took as she strode away from the ranch.

It wasn't until he could no longer see Miss Randall's hat bobbing down the lane that Cord had turned to face Bodie. His son had stopped smacking flies with the old mallet Everett had given to him just yesterday and stood with his bottom lip rolled out in a pout.

"Why's that mean lady mad at us, Daddy?" Bodie questioned. "Did I do something wrong?"

Cord shook his head and lifted Bodie in his arms, giving his son a hug. Sometimes he forgot just how young his little boy was, especially when he looked and generally acted older than his age.

"You didn't do anything wrong, Bode. She's just out of sorts, that's all. How about you help me with the colt, and then we'll wash up for supper?"

"Okay!" Bodie said, squirming to be set down.

Cord set him on his feet, took the mallet from Bodie, and left it on the porch, then they made their way over to the corral. He set Bodie on the top rail of the fence, where he'd be out of the way and safe, then returned to working with the colt.

As he worked, Cord glanced up at the blue sky overhead. He hoped the warm weather continued for a while. The weather had cooled down the first week of November but had warmed up so much the past few days, Cord hadn't even pulled on a coat to start the chores the past two mornings. Grateful for the pleasant temperatures that allowed his son to be outside and enjoying the fresh air while he worked, Cord thought how much easier it was to keep an eye, or ear, on Bodie when they could both be outdoors.

If the nice weather continued, Cord decided he might even have some of the hired hands help him install a new front walk when they got back tomorrow. He'd given his crew a few days off with pay after they'd driven several head of his cattle to the depot in Heppner to ship out. Impressed by how hard every hired man had worked all summer and fall, he felt it only right to give them the time off with pay as his way of saying thanks for their efforts.

Cord had felt both humbled and gratified when the cowboys who'd worked for Everett had agreed to stay on and work for him. They were a hardworking lot, and he could depend on them to do whatever was needed, even if it meant keeping an eye on Bodie for an hour or two.

After Cleo and Everett had moved into town, Bodie had spent a considerable amount of time in the bunkhouse with Tug, the foreman. The old cowboy was no longer able to ride, but he still oversaw the work each day and had taken over the duties of bunkhouse cook.

Eventually, Cord knew he'd need to hire a housekeeper and maybe a cook for the house. But for now, they made do. He and Bodie frequently ate in the bunkhouse with the cowboys.

Cord glanced over at his son as the colt ran in a circle around the corral. Bodie was sturdy and strong, but Cord didn't think he'd cause any damage with the mallet Everett had given to him to play with. As a preventative measure, Cord had gone over a list of things Bodie could hit with it, and things he could not. He didn't care if his son walloped the old hitching rail by the house that was one good windstorm away from falling down. It seemed to be Bodie's preferred place to swat at flies. He certainly wasn't hurting the uneven, chipped stones that served as the front walk across the yard.

Gracy Randall had no right to chastise the boy. None at all. Cord thought of a dozen things he should have said to her, but he'd been so taken aback by her presence, not to mention her comeliness, that he'd felt like a half-witted dunce from the moment she'd spun around and screeched at him.

"That's the way, Daddy. You got him now!" Bodie called encouragement, drawing Cord back to the moment. Perhaps his son was allowed to run a little wild from time to time, but it didn't mean he was undisciplined or unruly, or whatever other names that snippy woman had said.

Honestly, he just couldn't bend his thoughts around her being Cleo and Everett's beloved daughter. The way the two of them had spoken about her, she'd sounded like she was only one feather short of being a winged angel.

With that temper of hers and red hair, he would never have likened her to a celestial being. More like a gorgeous witch sent to bedevil him. He'd seen a photo of her taken when she'd graduated from high school, but the grainy image didn't do justice to her fine features or figure.

A sharp-tongued banshee she might be, but he couldn't deny she was pretty. The fact that he'd noticed made him even more determined to stay far away from the woman. After losing his beloved Helen, he had no interest in falling in love again. Besides, his wife hadn't even been gone two full years yet.

Cord thought of the January day he'd received a telegram from his sister at the hotel in New York where he'd been staying on one of his many business trips. The message had let him know Helen was terribly ill. Although Cord had caught the next train to Boston, by the time he'd journeyed home, Helen had been beyond saving. He'd held her in his arms as she'd drawn her last breath just moments after he'd arrived. The doctor hadn't been able to tell him exactly what was wrong, other than Helen's heart had just stopped functioning. Only two months after that, Cord's parents had been killed in an auto accident.

Lost in his grief, Cord had allowed Bodie any indulgence he'd wanted until Cornelia, his bossy sister, had taken matters in hand and assured him he'd ruin a perfectly good boy if he didn't get his head on straight.

So, Cord had tried. He'd done his best, but every time he thought he was making progress, something would remind him of his losses, and he'd begin the struggle all over again. That's when he'd landed on the idea of leaving Boston. Of course, he'd hated to move away from Cornelia and her family, but she'd understood.

Cord was thankful he'd moved to Hardman. He felt as though he and Bodie were finally beginning to thrive.

Then that tempestuous woman had to show up and shatter his hard-earned peace.

It would be tricky avoiding her, especially when he thought the world of Everett and Cleo, but he'd figure it out. He had to. Otherwise, he'd lose what little bit of sanity he had left around their defensive daughter.

Chapter Three

Weary, winded, and even more indignant by the time she reached Hardman, Gracy stood on the sidewalk and stared across the street at a lovely gray house with white trim surrounded by a white picket fence and a profusion of late-blooming autumn flowers. The wide porch steps appeared as welcoming as the slope of the roofline that almost looked like a smile.

The place was charming and inviting, and exactly the kind of house her mother would choose if she could pick a home, which, evidently, she had.

Gracy trudged across the street, through the open gate, down the paved walk, and up the steps. She stood outside the door, assured she'd found the right house by the rocking chairs sitting on either side of a little table she'd helped her mother paint the summer before she'd left home.

She could either knock on the door, face her parents, and find out what had inspired them to sell the ranch, or she could buy a stagecoach ticket headed back to Heppner and find a job somewhere other than Hardman.

However, the fact that her reticule and her money were sitting in Mr. Granger's entry left her without any choice but to stay in town. At least for tonight.

Gracy drew in a fortifying breath, lifted her hand, and rapped twice on the door with beautiful leaded glass insets.

Footsteps grew louder as they neared the portal; then the door swung open, and she stared at her mother. The woman appeared shocked, then overjoyed as recognition set in.

"Oh, Gracy! Oh, my sweet, sweet girl!" Cleo Randall wrapped Gracy in a tight hug that nearly left her breathless before she turned her loose. "What an unexpected gift to open the door and find you here. Come in, honey. Come in! I can't believe you're here!"

Gracy stepped into the house, admiring the light-drenched parlor decorated in hues of sage green, burgundy, and cream. She recognized their old sofa and chairs, but they had been reupholstered with a lovely floral tapestry material.

New lamps sat on end tables that had been refinished. Opposite the fireplace stood her grandmother's piano. Gracy walked over to it, yanked off her gloves, and ran her fingers across the keys.

She felt her mother slip an arm around her waist and lean her head against her shoulder. "It's been too long since you've played. I hope you'll entertain us soon with some songs."

"I will, Mama, but first, would you please explain why you and Papa sold the ranch to that dreadful, horrid Cord Granger and never mentioned a word about it to me?"

Her mother frowned. "Why in the world would you say that about Cord? He's the nicest young man, and we adore his son. Bodie is the sweetest little boy, full of hugs and giggles."

A picture of Cord as nice or Bodie as sweet failed to take shape in Gracy's mind. Rather than further debate the unpleasant man and his unruly son with her mother, she chose to focus on a more important matter.

"I had no idea you'd sold the ranch, Mama," Gracy said, aware her voice sounded whiny but incapable to do anything about it. Not when she felt like throwing a full-fledged temper fit. She drew in a breath and tried to gain control of her emotions. "I had the stagecoach let me off there. Mr. Granger and I had words. I walked into town, but I accidentally left my bag at the house."

"Oh, I'll telephone Cord and ask him to bring it in. He and Bodie can join us for supper."

"What?" Although she didn't intend to voice the question so loudly, Gracy's voice echoed off the walls. She wondered if her mother had heard a word she'd said. Gracy absolutely did not want to see

Cord Granger again, and she certainly held no interest in sitting at the same supper table with him. Not when her feet burned with blisters from walking in shoes meant only to look fashionable and her best hat now looked like something a wagon had run over.

Amid those turbulent thoughts, another surfaced. When, exactly, had her mother learned to use the telephone?

Gracey had spent the years since she'd left Hardman working as a telephone operator, and not once had her mother mentioned even the slightest interest in placing a call. Now she had her own telephone.

Overwhelmed and exhausted, Gracy felt on the verge of tears as her mother took her hand and led her through the house that was every bit as charming inside as it appeared outside. Proudly, her mother showed her the kitchen with an adjoining dining room, a screened-in porch, and even a bathroom, as well as a spacious bedroom on the main floor. Upstairs, there were two additional bedrooms. The moment she set foot in the light-drenched bedroom with a wide window seat overlooking the backyard, Gracy loved it. At the back of the yard was a small barn and corral, where three horses and a cow nibbled on the November grass. Grateful to see her parents hadn't sold her mare, Gracy looked forward to riding Cider soon. The sight of their old dog, Bentley, napping in a patch of sunshine made her smile.

"What do you think of our new home?" her mother asked, unable to hide her eagerness for Gracy's approval.

"It's wonderful, Mama. Your new home is lovely, and I can see it is much more suited to your tastes than the house on the ranch would ever be, but why did you sell? Why on earth didn't you say anything about it?"

Her mother sighed and walked over to the window seat, staring out the window for a long moment. "Your father and I are getting older, as you well know. After another winter of trying to keep up with everything, we decided it was time to do something different. We want to enjoy what years we have left instead of working ourselves to death. When Luke Granger mentioned his cousin was looking for a place to purchase, it just seemed like the perfect time to sell."

"But why keep it a secret? You could have told me," Gracy said, going to stand beside her mother. "I don't understand why you never said anything all this time. If I understood that deplorable Mr. Granger correctly, you sold the place to him back in the spring. Where did you live while this house was built?"

"I'm sorry, sweetheart. We never meant to exclude you from our plans. We didn't say anything because we knew how much you loved the ranch, Gracy. And if things were different, if life were different, we'd still be there with ..." Her mother snapped her mouth shut, then sighed. "Anyway, Cord allowed us to stay there while our house was constructed. I cooked and cleaned and watched

THE CHRISTMAS KISS

Bodie, while your father taught Cord all about the ranch in exchange for our room and board. It was a perfect arrangement for all of us, but I do so miss seeing Bodie every day."

"How could you possibly miss that … that … heathenish maker of mischief? He was beating the hitching rail to death and broke two of the stepping stones in the few minutes I was there."

"Cord is planning to move the hitching rail and put in a new fence in the spring. And he's going to replace the stones with a paved walk. That will be another project for spring, unless this nice weather continues to hold. Don't judge Cord or Bodie harshly. Life hasn't been easy on either of them." Cleo motioned for Gracy to follow her downstairs.

"Where's Papa?"

"At the newspaper office. He enjoys working with the printing machines and is quite good at keeping them running. I think he also enjoys being the first to find out the latest news from Tom Grove and the others who contribute articles. He'll be home in about an hour."

Gracy couldn't picture her father working in an office any more than she could imagine her parents happily living in town. Unable to absorb all the information she'd discovered since setting foot off the stagecoach, she just wanted to climb in bed and pretend this disastrous day had never happened.

"If you like it, the room with the window seat is yours for the length of your visit," her mother said as they walked into the kitchen. Cleo peeked into the oven, then stirred something in a pot simmering on the back of the stove. The steam that rose from it carried a hint of cinnamon and apples, making Gracy realize she'd skipped lunch and was starving.

"I adore the room, Mama." Gracy knew it was time to confess the truth about her reason for being in Hardman. "But I'm not here for a visit. I start a new job on Monday at the telephone office here in town. If you don't mind my living here with you for a while, until I find a place to rent, I'd like to stay with you and Papa."

Her mother squealed, flung the spoon from her hand into the sink, and wrapped her arms around Gracy. "Your father and I would be so, so happy to have you stay with us for as long as you like, honey. That's the best news I've had in a long, long time. After all that happened, I wasn't sure you'd ever return to Hardman."

"I know, Mama, but it's long past time for me to come home, even if home is now far different than I expected."

Cleo patted her cheek and offered her an indulgent smile. "Expectations are fickle things. Don't build your future or your dreams on them." Her mother wrinkled her nose and stepped back. "You need a bath, honey. Go take one, and I'll find a dress for you to wear until Cord brings your bag. Do you have trunks that need to be retrieved from the stage office?"

"No. They're arriving by freight wagon tomorrow."

Gracy removed her dusty hat, sat on a kitchen chair to tug off her shoes, and winced at the sight of blisters that had broken and bled all over her stockings.

"Oh, your poor feet!" Cleo glanced at them. "Once you get cleaned up, I have some salve I'll rub on them."

Gracy removed her dust-caked suit jacket, appalled at how dirty both it and she had gotten during her adventures of the day. She went into the bathroom and turned on the water in the bathtub, marveling at the wonders her parents had finally embraced, even though she never thought to see the day they'd live in a house with a telephone, electricity, and a bathroom, or in town, no less.

After soaking long enough for her fingers to wrinkle on the ends, she washed her hair, then drained the water. She sat on the edge of the tub wrapped in a fluffy towel that smelled of sunshine and Bee Soap, a laundry soap manufactured by the Colgate company that her mother favored. She'd just used a second towel to squeeze the moisture from her hair when she heard a tap on the door.

"Ready for clothes?" her mother asked as she opened the door and stepped inside.

"I am, Mama, and thank you. I feel so much better after washing away all that dirt and grime. This bathroom is divine."

"Glad you like it, honey." Cleo smiled at her. "You look refreshed, if not a little tired. Perhaps you should head to bed early tonight."

Gracy nodded as she eyed the dress her mother had carried over one arm. It wasn't an old chore dress but a gown she'd worn to a New Year's dance she'd attended before she'd left Hardman. The dark blue gown was embroidered with silver threads that had shimmered in the light and made her feel like a princess at a ball. For one magical evening, she'd danced for hours with her own Prince Charming.

"No, Mama. I'm not wearing that. I can't, and I won't do it!" she said vehemently. "If there's nothing else for me to wear, just bring me a robe, or even one of Papa's shirts and a pair of his pants, but I am not wearing that dress."

Cleo's eyes widened at Gracy's reaction to the gown, and she silently backed from the room. Gracy felt bad for speaking sharply to her mother, but the woman should have known Gracy had no interest in wearing the dress ever again.

She finished toweling her hair and used her mother's comb to work out the tangles. When Cleo reappeared in the doorway, she held a dark blue calico dress dotted with little pink rosebuds she'd made for Gracy when she'd been seventeen. She wasn't sure it would fit. Her figure had evolved since the carefree days of her youth.

"Thank you, Mama," Gracy said, smiling at her mother. Truthfully, her mother was hardly more than a stranger these days, connected by their past and the sporadic letters they exchanged. No wonder her mother had filled her letters these last many months with so much news of the town. It had been a means of hiding the truth about selling the ranch.

Angry and hurt, Gracy realized her mother could be experiencing some of the same feelings toward her. Gracy had arrived on her doorstep unannounced with plans to live with her parents for an indefinite period without mentioning a word about it in any of her recent letters. She'd been thinking about returning home for months and had finally made the decision three weeks ago when she'd heard about the opening at the telephone office in Hardman. Although it was painful to be in town, where memories assailed her, she'd just felt such an inexplicable, pressing need to return.

However, it had been childish of her to pretend everything in Hardman had stood still after she'd left, and would now resume as it had once been.

While she was being introspective, she admitted that she'd been unkind to Mr. Granger's little boy, even if the youngster did seem undisciplined. She'd also been rude to Mr. Granger, and that bothered her. Generally, she was a happy, considerate person, but the moment she'd seen the Granger boy bludgeoning the hitching post, she'd felt unmoored and lashed out in anger and fear.

"Mama, I'm sorry I didn't mention wanting to move back. I should have discussed it with you and Papa instead of assuming it would be fine for me to just show up and expect to live with you. I apologize. If my presence is an inconvenience, I can get a room at the hotel or the boarding house."

"Nonsense, honey. I'm thrilled you've finally come home to where you belong. You are welcome here for as long as you wish to stay. If you don't mind my asking, though, what made you decide to return to Hardman? You've been so ... strongly opinioned on the matter all these years." Cleo handed her a set of undergarments and a petticoat. "Why now?"

Gracy slipped on the cotton drawers and chemise, then held up her arms as her mother settled the petticoat over her head and tugged it into place around her waist.

"You've always had such a tiny waist. Not all women are fortunate enough to have no need for a corset to cinch them in," Cleo said with a hint of pride in her voice.

"Thank you, Mama. I think I got that from you since you look far younger than your age." If it weren't for her mother's silvery white hair, she could easily have been mistaken for a woman in her fifties instead of one who was seventy.

Gracy slipped her arms into the sleeves of the dress. "As to why I came back to Hardman, I don't know how to explain it, but I've recently experienced such an urgent need to be back here. It won't be easy, but being in Hardman feels right."

"I'm so glad, Gracy. So incredibly glad to have you here." Her mother gave her another hug, then stepped back, offering her a teasing grin. "That looks perfect."

Gracy tugged at the overly tight bodice and gave her mother a disparaging glance. "I'm afraid to ask perfect for what, Mama. It's way too tight."

"Oh, bosh." Cleo waved a dismissive hand at her. "That dress was always so pretty on you. With your beautiful hair and that pale, flawless skin, you are just a picture of prettiness."

"When you put it like that, how could I possibly wear anything else this evening?" Gracy smiled. "I really am happy for you and Papa, but it will take some getting used to, no longer being at the ranch."

"I know, baby, but we still have some of the horses, and Cord would be happy for a visit anytime."

An unladylike snort rolled out of Gracy. "I highly doubt that, but I do look forward to riding Cider soon."

Cleo opened a mirrored medicine cabinet set into the wall above the sink and took out a little tin of salve. "Rub that on your blisters. If you're warm enough, don't bother with stockings and shoes. The air will do those blisters some good. When you finish, come into the kitchen. You can help me set the table."

"Yes, ma'am." Gracy took the tin and perched on the edge of the bathtub again to rub the salve on her blisters. After returning it to the cabinet, she washed her hands and studied her reflection in the mirror. Since her hair was still damp, she left it down, knowing her parents wouldn't care if it wasn't properly styled while they ate dinner. She made a silly face, then rushed to the kitchen to help her mother.

She'd just reached for a stack of plates when the back door opened and her father stepped inside.

"It's still unbelievably warm out there, Cleo. I can't imagine what Mother Nature is thinking with this mild weather, but I won't argue with her. I can't remember it ever being this warm in November." His back was to them as he hung his jacket and hat on hooks by the door.

"It has been a strange month," Cleo said, pointing a finger from Gracy to her husband.

SHANNA HATFIELD

Gracy placed her finger to her lips, and her mother winked at her, nodding encouragingly. On silent feet, she crept across the floor until she was only a foot away from her father. When he turned around, Gracy threw her hands in the air and yelled "surprise!"

His startled expression made both Gracy and Cleo laugh, then Everett whooped and wrapped his arms around his daughter, lifting her off her feet as he hugged her and kissed her cheek.

"Oh, my lands, Gracy. You pert near made my heart stop, you little stinker. How long have you been here?"

"Only about an hour or so," Gracy said, giving her father another tight hug before he set her down and stepped back.

"You get prettier every time we see you."

"You always say that, Papa." Gracy gave him a cheeky grin. "Feel free to continue."

He chuckled and took her hand in his, spinning her around. "You really are a lovely woman, Gracy, and I'm excited to have you home." He frowned. "But I guess you figured out home is no longer the ranch."

"She and Cord had a little set-to," Cleo tattled. "Your daughter looked mad enough to chew nails when she got here."

Everett laughed and patted Gracy on the shoulder. "Your mother used to make me want to yank my hair out when we were just getting acquainted. Cord's one of the finest young men I've had the pleasure of knowing. Give him a chance,

Gracy, my girl. You might find he's not nearly as horrible as you currently believe."

Gracy wondered how her father had always been able to read her mind so well. It appeared the years hadn't dimmed his abilities. It wasn't like she hadn't seen her parents at all since she left Hardman. They generally came to visit her for her birthday in May, and they'd come to Grass Valley three times for Christmas.

Thoughts of Christmas at the ranch with the holiday decorations set out and the delicious aromas emanating from the kitchen as she and her mother baked all of Papa's favorite treats had made her eager to return home.

Now, though, it wouldn't be the same. Perhaps not terrible, but definitely different.

Chapter Four

Cord turned the colt loose in the pasture connected to the corral, then reached out a hand to his son.

"Want a ride?" he asked, grinning at Bodie as he swung the boy up to his shoulders.

Bodie smiled broadly, resting one small hand on top of Cord's hat, while the other clung to his index finger. "I like rides, Daddy."

"Did I know that?" Cord asked, pretending to be uncertain.

"Yes!" Bodie giggled, tapping his feet against Cord's chest. "You're silly, Daddy."

"So you've mentioned before." Cord swung Bodie down and handed him a little bucket. Bodie went to feed the chickens, while Cord milked the cows and fed the horses. After completing the evening chores, the two of them wiped their feet on the mat at the back door and went inside.

"How does leftover stew sound? We still have some from the pot Cleo sent out yesterday." Cord glanced at Bodie as he scrubbed his hands at the kitchen sink.

"I like stew," Bodie said, then hopped on one foot from one black tile to another, doing his best to avoid stepping on the white tiles. It was a game the boy enjoyed playing on the black and white floor whenever they were in the kitchen.

Cord dried his hands on a clean towel, swept up Bodie, and held him at the sink so he could wash his hands.

"Scrub them good," Cord said as Bodie rubbed soap over his fingers and splashed in the water. By the time the boy finished, Cord's shirt was half-soaked, but at least Bodie's hands were clean.

Cord gave him a towel to dry his hands, then took the stew from the refrigerator. He would warm it along with slices of bread he'd picked up yesterday at the Decker's bakery in town for dinner. Before he could spoon the stew into a pan to heat, the telephone jangled.

"Can I answer?" Bodie asked, racing across the kitchen to where the phone was fastened to the wall by the hallway door.

"You may. Use your manners." Cord hid a grin as Bodie answered the telephone.

"Hello! This is Bodie, I mean Juniper Creek Ranch. Hi!"

Cord listened to the one-sided conversation, deducing from Bodie's comments it was Cleo.

"Grammy wants to talk to you, Daddy," Bodie said, holding out the earpiece.

Cord thought it was wonderful the way Everett and Cleo had encouraged Bodie to refer to them as Grammy and Gramps. His son couldn't remember his grandparents, but he adored Cleo and Everett.

Cord set the stew on the counter, then moved over to the phone.

"Evening, Cleo. Might I assume your daughter arrived?"

"She did. I don't know what was said, but she looks mad enough to spew venom."

Cord tried to swallow a chuckle but failed. "I wouldn't doubt it. What can I do for you?"

"Well, it seems she left in such a fit of agitation, she forgot her bag at your house. She doesn't have a thing with her. I'd be so grateful if you could bring it in. And since you'd be here anyway, we'd love to have you stay for supper. I made a beef roast with all the trimmings and the vanilla cake you like so much."

His mouth started to water at the thought of one of Cleo's incredible meals. Even though he loathed the very notion of seeing Gracy Randall again, Cord found he couldn't refuse the invitation. Perhaps Gracy would be so worn out from her travels and tormenting him, she'd sleep through dinner.

When he didn't reply right away, Cleo sighed. "I'm sure Gracy probably reacted badly to finding strangers in the ranch house. She always did have a temper when riled. Please don't judge her too harshly until you've seen her at her best. I have a feeling you got a clear view of her at her worst."

"She does seem to have a temper," he said with a grin. "We'll bring in her bag. Are you eating at the usual time?"

"We are. Everett should be home soon, and he has no idea Gracy is here. If you hurry, you might even get to see his reaction to her unexpected visit."

"We'll wash up and head into town."

"Wonderful. See you soon. And thank you, Cord."

"Of course, Cleo."

Cord hung up the phone, returned the stew to the refrigerator, then removed his filthy shirt.

"Are we going somewhere?" Bodie asked as Cord toed off his boots and unfastened his jeans. "We are, son. How about you go comb your hair?"

"Okay, Daddy!" Bodie raced out of the room, and Cord could hear him pounding upstairs to his bedroom. By the time Cord had washed his face and changed into clean clothes, Bodie had returned with his hair still dripping water and his cowlick sticking up by his left temple.

"Hey, pardner. Let's dry you off a bit before we go." Cord took a towel and rubbed it over Bodie's head, making him giggle, then used his comb to style his son's hair. He helped Bodie change into a clean shirt and pants, then held his coat while the little boy rammed his arms into the sleeves.

"I need my hat, Daddy," Bodie said, pointing to the hook that held his little cowboy hat.

"I think we'd better leave that home tonight, son. It feels like it might be chilly this evening, so you'd best wear this one instead." Cord took a knit cap, one Cleo had made for Bodie, and settled it on his head.

Rather than his cowboy hat, Cord pulled on a woolen driving cap, then slipped on his coat. "Ready?" he asked Bodie.

"Yep!" the child proclaimed and started to open the back door.

"Oh, I forgot something," Cord said, hurrying into the front entry, where he found a large traveling bag that felt like the woman had packed it full of bricks. It was probably a good thing Gracy had gotten so riled she'd forgotten it. He couldn't imagine her lugging it all the way into town.

A prick of guilt niggled him that he hadn't offered her a ride into Hardman, but she'd made him so upset—left him so agitated—he could hardly think straight.

He didn't like the feeling, and he didn't particularly like her.

"Come on, Daddy!" Bodie called, racing ahead to the carriage house Cord had hired a crew to build just before the new Staver Runabout automobile he'd ordered had arrived in September. The vehicle included all the features Cord had sought, including a full windshield across the front. Bodie liked the deep Christmas red color. Since the auto was trimmed in brass with white-painted wheels, his son had dubbed it Peppermint.

Cord pushed open the door, and Bodie ran inside the building, climbing into the auto. He'd taught his son how to work the controls so he could help him start it. The auto sputtered to life, then

Cord climbed behind the wheel and drove out of the building, heading toward town.

It didn't take long before he turned down the street where Cleo and Everett lived. The couple had been able to purchase a large lot that gave them room for a small pasture and a barn for their horses and milk cow. Cleo also raised chickens.

Cord waved to Percy and Brynn Bruner as they strolled up their front walk, then he turned around and parked in front of the Randall home. The cottage-style house always looked so friendly and inviting.

He knew Cleo was excited to festoon the front porch for Christmas with garlands and bows. Cord wondered if he could talk her into coming out to the ranch to help deck his halls. He'd brought one trunk full of sentimental decorations with him, but he needed to purchase more. He added that to his mental list of things to attend to later as he hopped out of the auto and picked up Gracy's bag.

Bodie ran ahead, then stopped when a rock caught his eye. Cord grinned at him and continued up the steps, then rang the bell.

"Look at my rock, Daddy!" Bodie held it up, and Cord admired the oval shape, pointing out the veins running through it as they waited for someone to open the door.

"Are you going to add it to your collection?" Cord asked, ringing the bell again.

"I am. I ..."

The door swung open, and Cord gaped at Gracy. Her hair was down, surrounding her face and flowing over her shoulders in thick, fragrant waves that looked like they'd been touched with fire in the light provided by the wall sconces behind her. She wore a dress that made her eyes seem bluer and her cheeks pinker while hugging her curves to the point he couldn't help but gape at her fine figure. He certainly hadn't been fully aware of her decadent form earlier when she'd worn the loose suit jacket over her traveling attire.

As she shifted from one foot to the other, he saw bare toes peeking out from the hem of her dress and would have commented on it, but Bodie suddenly erupted in tears. Not just a silent tear or two, but all-out screams of terror. He dropped his rock, wrapped his arms around Cord's leg, and buried his face against his thigh, sobbing hysterically.

"Hey. Here now." Cord practically tossed the bag to Gracy, then lifted Bodie in his arms, rubbing his hands comfortingly up and down his son's back. "What's wrong, Bode? Hmm? Did something bite you?"

"No!" Bodie wailed as he clung to Cord, rubbing his face against his neck. "It's her. The mean lady who yelled at me. She's scary, Daddy! She's scary!"

Cord edged past Gracy as she stared at him, clutching her bag to her chest. The color drained from her face, and she looked a little woozy as she backed up a few paces.

"What's all the caterwauling about?" Everett asked as he hastened into the entry.

"The mean lady yelled at me!" Bodie wailed, holding out his arms to Everett.

"She did, did she?" Everett asked, giving Gracy a fatherly scowl. "Well, that wasn't very nice of her, was it?"

Bodie shook his head and sniffled, the tears beginning to recede.

Cleo pulled off Bodie's stocking cap and brushed his bangs out of his eyes with a gentle hand. "Now why in the world would she yell at a sweet boy like you?"

Bodie shrugged his little shoulders. "I was just smacking those ol' flies with your mallet, Gramps."

"You were? Did you get a bunch of them?" Everett asked with an indulgent look.

"I sure did. They went splat!" Bodie smacked his hands together.

"Well, how about that!" Everett jiggled Bodie in his arms, bringing out his smile. Cord removed his son's coat, glad the storm of tears had already abated. His little boy loved Cleo and Everett, but if seeing Gracy made him cry, he couldn't imagine they'd be spending much time together in the future, at least while the exasperating woman was in town.

"Do you think the mean lady should apologize to you?" Cleo asked, frowning at her daughter while motioning her forward.

"Yes," Bodie said, giving Cleo an earnest look. "My daddy makes me polyguys when I do something naughty."

Cleo set a hand on Gracy's shoulder and nudged her closer to Bodie and Everett. "Bodie, I'd like you to meet my daughter, Gracy. Gracy, this is Bodie Granger and his father, Cord."

Gracy swallowed hard, while her hands fidgeted with the handle of the bag she still held. "I'm terribly sorry for what occurred earlier today, Bodie. I was mean and scary and unforgivably rude. Please accept my apologies for speaking out of turn and any distress I caused by my insensitive, thoughtless actions."

Although she kept her focus on Bodie, Cord got the distinct feeling the words were meant for him.

Bodie stared at her for a long moment, then he slowly grinned. "You're pretty, but your hair looks like it's on fire, just like Mr. Bruner's!"

Gracy lifted a hand to her head, and the blush on her cheeks deepened. Cord wondered if she'd forgotten she wore it down.

"I suppose it does," she said, taking a long step back, looking for all the world like she wanted to escape.

"Come on, honey, you can help me finish dishing up supper," Cleo said, grabbing onto Gracy's arm and propelling her toward the kitchen.

Everett grinned and gave Bodie another pat on the back before setting him on his feet, then reached out to shake Cord's hand. "Thank you for bringing in Gracy's bag. I apologize for whatever transpired this afternoon out at the ranch. I feel like I'm to blame. I knew Gracy wouldn't take the sale of Juniper Creek well, which is the reason we avoided telling her. I should have told her months ago about selling it to you, so please accept my sincere regrets."

"Don't trouble yourself over it, Everett. I'm sure it was mostly a misunderstanding," Cord said, hesitating to relay to a man he thought of as a father figure and a friend that his daughter had behaved like a raging harridan. She had clearly terrified Bodie, although his son hadn't acted concerned about her earlier. Then again, Cord had no idea what, exactly, she'd said to the boy.

He supposed it was best to forget it had ever happened. Nothing good would come of harboring ill feelings toward Gracy Randall. Especially not when the sight of her had left his mouth so dry, he could hardly swallow.

How could a woman he'd despised so thoroughly upon their initial meeting now leave him so utterly intrigued?

Even more unsettling was his growing interest in her. Cord knew nothing, not a single good thing, could come of it. Gracy Randall was an opinionated menace, and the sooner she returned to Grass Valley, the happier he'd be.

Chapter Five

"I'm sure I misunderstood what you said, Mrs. Mussner. Would you please repeat it?" Gracy stood in the telephone office on the verge of a ... she wasn't sure what, but she felt like her world teetered on the edge of imploding.

"I do apologize, dear. In all the flurry of activity and the upcoming holidays, it simply slipped my mind to let you know the position was no longer available," said the telephone office manager.

Betty Mussner had been in charge of the telephone office from the day it had opened a few years ago. Gracy had known the widow woman for years. Betty's daughter had been a few years ahead of Gracy in school, and she'd liked the Mussner family, which was one more reason she'd felt confident in her decision to return to Hardman.

She'd heard one of the telephone operators was planning to move away right before Thanksgiving, leaving an opening that Gracy was all too eager to fill.

Only, it seemed the girl had called off her wedding, and, out of loyalty, Mrs. Mussner had allowed her to keep her job. That was all fine and good, but it left Gracy without any source of employment. She had no intention of sitting around, twiddling her thumbs, waiting for a storybook hero to sweep her off her feet and profess his undying love.

She'd been in love once. Samuel Marsh had been so shy, he'd barely managed to ask her to accompany him to a church picnic. But he had, and she'd gone, and they'd fallen in love immediately. He'd been new to Hardman and, because of his reserved nature, found it challenging to make new friends.

Gracy had been in her last year of high school and was friendly with most everyone. They'd courted all autumn and enjoyed a lovely Christmas together at the ranch, and then they'd gone to the New Year's Eve dance. Samuel had proposed when he'd brought her home, and Gracy had accepted without a moment of hesitation. They'd made plans to wed in June after she graduated from school, only Samuel had died of the influenza that had claimed far too many people that winter.

Gracy had lost not only Samuel, but also her lone sibling, Rob, and his sweet, precious family had all died too. Although Gracy had gotten sick, it had been a mild case. She'd nursed her parents and some of the ranch hands, unaware that Rob's family had even taken ill until it had been too late. And poor Samuel. He'd been all alone in his home just a few blocks from the doctor's office.

The losses and grief had driven Gracy to leave town. Memories had haunted her around every corner, and she hadn't been able to bear to be there a day longer. So, she'd packed a trunk with her things, and set out to make her own way after acquiring a position at the Grass Valley telephone office. She'd been happy there all these years and shared a small house with a widow who worked in the hotel's kitchen. Yet, the moment the notion popped into her head to return to Hardman, it had felt right. It was as though she'd had to go away long enough for the pain to subside and the harsh memories to dim.

But part of the reason she'd felt good about returning was the promise of a job she could do blindfolded.

"Are you certain you have no position open for me, Mrs. Mussner? I gave up my job and my house and moved here on your word that I would have employment."

The older woman nodded her head. "I know, dear. I know. Oh, mercy me! I can't imagine how I let myself get into such a pickle. I do apologize, Gracy, but there is nothing currently available for you here." Mrs. Mussner did appear apologetic, but it didn't make Gracy feel any better.

"If a position opens, would you please let me know?" Gracy forced herself to smile although she felt more like kicking something.

"Of course, Gracy! Of course, I will." Mrs. Mussner walked with her to the door. "Oh, I just had a thought. I heard George and Aleta Bruner may be looking for a little help during the holiday season. I know it isn't what you intended to do, but you might stop by the store."

"I will, Mrs. Mussner. Thank you." Gracy tipped her head to the woman, then hurried outside. Intent on heading straight to the mercantile, she hastened up the street, then raced around the corner. She smacked into someone and would have fallen backward if hands hadn't grabbed her elbows and kept her upright.

She glanced up into the face of Cord Granger. It was a pity such a handsome face belonged to such an exasperating man.

He raised his eyebrows as he stared at her but didn't turn her loose.

"Oh, it's you," she said, wondering what it was about him that made her feel so unlike herself. Her heart fluttered rapidly while her palms grew damp and her mind swirled with thoughts better left alone.

"That it is, Miss Randall. Where were you off to in such a rush?"

"The mercantile. I heard they might be hiring." Gracy took a step back, forcing him to let go of her. Something about being close to him with his hands touching her even through her jacket left her befuddled, and she didn't like it. Not one bit.

Cord frowned and tipped his black cowboy hat back on his head, drawing her attention to his thick brown hair. If he let it grow longer, she was sure it would curl. The last thing she needed was another reason to be attracted to the man. One she hadn't yet decided she liked.

"I thought you were starting work this morning at the telephone office," Cord said. "Do you need a second job?"

"No. The position I was promised is no longer available. The girl who was leaving the telephone office didn't. Mrs. Mussner feels duty-bound to allow her to keep her job. It leaves me seeking gainful employment."

"That seems unfair since you moved back to fill that position." Cord took a step to the side. "I hope you find something you enjoy, Miss Randall."

"Thank you." She moved past him, then turned back, uncertain why she felt the need to prolong their conversation. "It was nice to share supper with you the other evening. I am truly sorry for upsetting Bodie. It deeply disturbed me to realize just the sight of me made him scared. I would never willingly frighten a child, although that seems to be exactly what I did, and I regret it more than words can express. That afternoon was not my finest moment, but it isn't any excuse. I do apologize, again, for saying things I had no right to say, or even think."

"Apology accepted. Bodie seemed to warm up to you after dinner when you played the piano and invited him to sit beside you. It was nice to hear you play." He glanced away and cleared his throat, then rubbed a hand across the back of his neck before he looked at her again. "I believe I also owe you an apology for saying a few things I shouldn't have."

"I'm sure I provoked you beyond reason, Mr. Granger. My mother has always said I possessed a rare talent for it, but thank you. Shall we begin anew, sir?"

Cord grinned and held out a hand. "Howdy, Miss Randall. I'm Cord Granger. I purchased Juniper Creek Ranch and think the world of your folks. I hope we'll be friends because my little boy loves your mom and dad as though they were his grandparents."

Gracy took his hand and smiled. "It's a pleasure to meet you, Mr. Granger. I hope you enjoy the ranch as much as I always did. I'm delighted your son and my parents have such a special bond. They needed that after we lost my brother and his family. They've missed the grandchildren so much, and I have too."

Cord's expression changed to one of sympathy. "I'm sorry for your losses, Miss Randall. It's hard to lose a loved one, and even harder to move beyond the grief. I know from experience."

She placed a hand on his arm and gazed into his face, surprised by the raw emotion that shimmered in his hazel eyes. Eyes that had the darkest, thickest lashes surrounding them. "I'm very sorry about your wife and parents. Mama told me what happened. It must have been terribly trying to get through all that and take care of Bodie."

"It was tough, and if it weren't for my sister setting me on my ear, Bodie might be running around as wild and uncivilized as you first assumed."

Gracy grinned. "Again, my apologies for being so … difficult upon our first meeting."

"Remember, we haven't met before today," he said, winking at her.

For some crazy reason, his playful attention made her stomach feel like butterflies were taking flight inside it. "I appreciate that, Mr. Granger, and your willingness to give me a second chance."

"I feel the same way." He leaned closer to her and lowered his voice slightly. "I do have one request, though."

"Yes?" she asked, admiring his smile and wondering what it would be like to be kissed by lips that looked so warm and firm. Annoyed with herself for her wayward thoughts, she forced her gaze to his eyes once again.

"I'd sure like it if you'd call me Cord instead of Mr. Granger. With Luke living here too, it could get confusing."

"Oh, I'm not sure that would be entirely proper," Gracy said, taking a step back before she gave in to the sudden, demanding urge to run her fingers over Cord's chin. Dark stubble covered his face and she wanted to know what it felt like. If it would be bristly or soft.

"Well, shoot! Here I thought kinda proper would be good enough," he teased, then he took her hand between both of his, giving it a gentle squeeze. "Please, Gracy? Would you call me Cord? I'm not one for a bunch of formality, even if Aunt Dora would explain in painstaking detail why I should follow all the appropriate guidelines of society."

"I do believe your aunt is far too occupied with her grandchildren and her new husband to pay much attention to something as trivial as the use of first names."

"True." He glanced at a watch he pulled from his vest pocket, snapped the lid closed, and tucked it back inside, then offered her a curious look. "Would you hold any interest in accompanying me to the opera house for a concert on Friday evening? I heard the group of singers is well-known around the Northwest."

Gracy had no intention of accompanying him anywhere, but apparently, her brain forgot to relay that news to her mouth. "Yes! I'd love to," she blurted, then gave Cord a sheepish look. "I mean, it sounds like a pleasant evening. Will Bodie join us?"

"No. It's probably best if he stays at Luke and Filly's house. He loves playing with Patrick, and Maura keeps a good eye on the younger ones." He backed up a step. "Would you like to have dinner before we go to the performance? We could eat at the restaurant if you like."

"Why don't you come over for dinner? Mama and Papa are always so happy to see you."

"That sounds good to me. I'll see you Friday." He tipped his hat to her and then continued on his way.

Gracy nodded and watched as he jogged across the street. What had she done, agreeing to go with him to a concert? That smacked of acceptance and possibly even courting. Then again, Cord didn't act as though he was interested in her *that* way. Perhaps the invitation was his way of building on the tenuous friendship they'd just established. That seemed the most reasonable explanation for the invitation.

"Enjoying the view?" a voice asked from beside her, startling her from her musings.

Gracy spun around and glowered at Brynn Bruner. She'd known the girl in school. Brynn was the kind of person everyone liked. Gracy was so pleased to see the vibrant young woman and Percy had found their way to each other. The few times she'd seen them together, they both looked thoroughly besotted even though they'd been married nearly a year.

Feigning ignorance, Gracy motioned across the street to a business owner hanging garland from his eaves. "The town does look quite festive with the decorations already going up."

Brynn playfully swatted her arm and fell into step with her as they walked toward the mercantile. "That isn't what I meant, and you know it, Gracy Randall. I was referring to Cord Granger. There isn't a single woman in town who hasn't tried to catch his eye, and just between us, I think a few who are taken have been eyeing him too. Until you came along, he acted as though he were blind, deaf, and dumb where the females of Hardman were concerned."

"Really?" Gracy asked, doing her best to sound disinterested, even though she wanted to hear more. "He hasn't courted anyone?"

"No. Everyone talks about how he must still be mourning his wife. I think he is, somewhat, but I've also noticed he's changed significantly since he came to Hardman. When he first arrived in town, he rarely smiled and walked with his shoulders hunched, like the weight he bore was too great to carry. The past few months, he's been full of smiles. I even heard him whistling when he and Bodie left Granger House after Thanksgiving dinner."

"It's wonderful he's finding his joy again," Gracy said, pondering if she'd found hers. She thought she had, but now that she was back in Hardman, she wasn't certain. While it felt right to be here, it had been hard to walk through town and see places that reminded her of the people she'd lost—those she'd once loved so unwaveringly. She had noticed her parents seemed so much more relaxed and at peace in their new home than they had since Rob and Julie and the children had died. She wasn't certain if it was selling the ranch, getting away from the memories there, or just beginning a new chapter in their lives that had made them more joyful.

In fact, Gracy thought her father, with his white hair and beard, would make a perfect Santa Claus, and her mother would make a lovely Mrs. Claus. She wondered if they could be talked into playing those characters for one of the events in town, such as the skating party, or perhaps the annual Christmas Carnival held at Dora Granger Rutherford's home. She decided to give it more thought later.

"Are you heading to the store, or out running errands?" Gracy asked Brynn as they darted between a wagon and an auto on their way across the street and then continued toward the mercantile. Brynn managed her grandfather's bookstore, and Percy operated a photography studio in the rooms above it.

"I had a few errands to run, and Percy asked me to deliver some photographs. The weather is so pleasant today, I admit I've been dawdling out in the sunshine. Grandpa and Dora are minding the store and told me not to rush, so I haven't. I thought you were starting work this morning at the telephone office?"

Gracy sighed. "I was supposed to, but Minerva Hadley called off her wedding and won't be leaving after all. Mrs. Mussner felt it only right to allow Minerva to continue in the position."

"I understand her point, but it still seems so unfair. What will you do?" Brynn asked as they stopped outside Bruner's Mercantile. Brynn's mother-in-law, Aleta, waved to them from the large display window, where she took down autumn decorations, no doubt in preparation for installing a holiday display.

"I heard your in-laws might be hiring."

Brynn's brow puckered in a frown. "They haven't mentioned anything to us, but that doesn't necessarily mean they aren't. If you are desperate for a job, I could use some assistance, just for a few days, while I set up my holiday displays. Usually, Percy helps me, but he's leaving tomorrow for Portland and will be gone for a week."

"Is he taking photos or talking about them?" Gracy had heard through her mother that Percy had started teaching photography classes a few times a year at a university in Portland.

"Both," Brynn said with a grin. "He promised the newspaper he'd cover a cattleman's meeting while he's there as well as some political gathering. He thought it would be a good opportunity for his students to practice."

"That's wonderful, Brynn. I'm so happy for you and Percy. After all that happened and Percy left town, I'm so glad he found his way home and to you."

Brynn's eyes glistened with unshed tears, and her face softened. "I'm grateful every day for it." She drew in a long breath, then took a few steps back. "I must get going, but if you can't find other employment, I could keep you busy for a few days."

"Thank you, Brynn. I might just take you up on that."

Gracy waved to her friend, then hurried inside the store. She sniffed deeply, inhaling the familiar scents that carried her back to her childhood. Although the inside of the store had been updated and changed, the friendly warmth of George and Aleta Bruner remained the same.

"Gracy! What brings you in?" Aleta asked, giving her a hug and a questioning glance before she moved back over to the display window, where she placed colorful paper leaves in a box.

"I heard you might be hiring and came to apply for a job."

Aleta appeared confused as she stood with a leaf in each hand. "I thought you were going to work at the telephone office. Was I mistaken?"

"No. I uh ... it seems Minerva Hadley called off her wedding. Mrs. Mussner felt it only right to allow her to keep her position."

"Oh, that's terrible, both to her wedding being called off and your being out of a job." Aleta placed the leaves in the box and picked up a few stragglers from the display. "George and I are fully staffed through the holidays, but if you want to work for a day or two, I could use temporary help. We gave our staff time off for Thanksgiving, and they won't be back until Wednesday. I could put you to work today and tomorrow if that might be of interest to you."

"I would like that very much, Mrs. Bruner. I need to keep busy. Perhaps with so many of the community members coming through the store, I'll hear of the possibility of an open position elsewhere in town."

Aleta smiled at her. "Wonderful. Let's get an apron for you, and then you can help me with the displays. And please, call me Aleta."

"I will, Mrs. Bruner, I mean, Aleta. Thank you so much."

By Tuesday evening, Aleta had taught Gracy everything she knew about arranging displays. While it wasn't the job she'd planned to do, Gracy had enjoyed the work and getting to know George and Aleta Bruner better. It amazed her how different everyone in town seemed since she saw them as an adult instead of looking through the lens of a child or young girl.

She spent the remainder of the week helping Brynn with the displays in her store. They proved to be even more fun than working at the mercantile since she and Brynn walked home together at the end of the day.

Friday evening, she'd just waved to Brynn and started up the walk to her parents' home when the door opened, and her mother frantically waved at her.

Gracy lifted her skirt and took the porch steps in two strides. "What's wrong? Did Papa get hurt? Are you well?"

Cleo nodded. "Yes, we're fine, but you're going to be late. Cord will be here in an hour for dinner, then we're all going to the concert. Did you forget?"

Gracy groaned. "It completely slipped my mind." She'd been so busy working at jobs so unfamiliar to her, she had somehow forgotten about accompanying Cord to the opera house that night.

"Hurry! I drew a bath for you. You've got time to clean up and change if you rush. I'll style your hair for you," Cleo said, giving her a shove down the hall.

Gracy might have argued with her, but she knew she had cobwebs in her hair from climbing into the attic at the bookstore to help Brynn bring down more Christmas decorations. Without wasting a moment, she flung off her coat, kicked off her shoes, and was soon in the steamy water of the deep bathtub, using a bar of Cashmere Bouquet soap to wash away the cares of the day. Not taking time to linger, she quickly washed her hair and toweled it mostly dry, pulled on the clean undergarments her mother had left for her in the room, slipped on her robe, then raced upstairs to dress.

Much to her dismay, her mother had pressed the dark blue velvet gown embellished with silver threads for Gracy to wear. Gracy was certain she'd made it perfectly clear she had no interest in ever wearing the dress again, but something about it called to her. Would wearing it ruin her evening with Cord? Or would it help her move past one more painful memory she'd procrastinated working through?

Aware of her mother's tenacity when it came to getting her way once she'd made up her mind, Gracy slipped on the gown, enjoying the feel of the soft fabric against her skin. The velvet dress was the nicest garment she'd ever owned. The silver embroidery pattern of a simple leaf and vine design glistened against the deep blue fabric.

Gracy slipped her feet into a pair of black leather shoes with French heels, double straps, and an embellishment of a few jet beads sewn in a diamond pattern on the toe.

Even with her hair waving around her face, she felt almost regal.

"Are you dressed?" Cleo asked as she rapped once on the door, then charged into the room.

Gracy rose from the chair she'd sat in to put on the shoes and held her hands out at her sides. "Really, Mama? You are going to make me wear this dress?"

"I am, for several reasons, not the least of which is it looks beautiful on you. I also think until you wear it again, you won't be able to disassociate it from that night with Samuel. Perhaps you don't want to, and that's fine too, honey. I just thought it would be good for you to wear it tonight. After all, you and Cord have both made it clear you're nothing more than friends, so what could it hurt?"

"I suppose nothing," Gracy said, unconvinced her mother wasn't plotting something, but she had no time to worry about it. With her mother's help, they managed to subdue her hair into a popular pompadour with soft waves in the front and a few curling tendrils framing her face.

Cleo pinned a dark blue silk rose in Gracy's hair and stepped back. "Now, that's lovely. You are just such a beautiful girl, my darling daughter, but don't let it go to your head."

Gracy laughed and hugged her mother. "I won't. Do you need help with dinner?"

"Gracious, no. I don't want to chance you spilling anything on your dress. Why don't you get out your black cape to wear and leave it by the door with your opera bag? By then, your father should be home and Cord will be arriving."

"Sure, Mama. Thank you." Gracy gathered what she would need for the evening, left the bag, her cape, and a pair of gloves in a chair in the front room, then started down the hall just as the doorbell rang. She opened it to find Cord standing on the other side, looking quite dashing in a dark gray suit, white shirt, and a blue tie that was almost the same color as her gown. He whipped off a gray Homburg hat and tipped his head to her.

A slow, easy smile tilted his lips upward as he seemed to study her from the top of her head to the tips of her shoes peeking beneath the hem of her gown.

"Evening, Gracy," he said in that deep, rich voice that made warmth curl through her.

Friends! We're just friends! she reminded herself as she stepped back and he walked past her, filling her nose with the scent of woods, spice, and virile man.

Chapter Six

Cord took a shallow breath, trying not to inhale another whiff of Gracy's sensual floral scent. He had no idea what she was wearing, but it had tantalized his senses the moment he'd stepped past her when she'd opened the door to allow him inside her parents' home.

He sat across from her at the dinner table, unable to enjoy Cleo's fine meal of roasted chicken with seasoned rice, canned green beans, and hot rolls dripping with butter and peach preserves. Everett talked about the printing machine at the newspaper office he'd worked on that afternoon, but he might as well have been speaking in a foreign tongue for all the attention Cord paid to him.

It was impossible to focus on anything except Gracy. Cord had fixated on how glorious she appeared the moment she'd opened the door. The gown she wore was such a dark shade of blue and looked so soft—so touchable—he mused that the fabric might have been woven from fibers snatched right out of a deep winter night sky. Tiny, shimmery silver threads adorned the velvet dress, refracting the light every time she moved and drawing his gaze back to her no matter how hard he tried to look away.

The meal seemed to last forever, especially when Cord could hardly swallow past the lump that had inexplicably filled his throat. Was he coming down with something? Surely not. He was rarely ever sick. But what was causing his loss of appetite, and why did he feel both feverish and chilled?

Cord forced himself to take another bite of chicken and broke off a piece of the roll, shoving it into his mouth.

"Another fine, fine meal, wife," Everett said, leaning back in his chair and patting his stomach.

"It's delicious, as always," Cord hurried to agree, although the food could have tasted like sawdust or pasteboard, and he likely wouldn't have noticed. Although he spoke to Cleo, he continued studying the woman seated across from him.

Gracy noticed his gaze on her and dropped her eyes to her nearly empty plate.

"If you men are finished, Gracy and I will see to the dishes, then we can be on our way. Everett, darling, didn't you say you had something you wanted to ask Cord about investments or banking?"

"I did." Everett rose from the table and motioned to Cord. "Let's go to the front room."

Cord wiped his mouth on his napkin and followed as Everett led the way from the dining room. He glanced over his shoulder and saw Gracy sweep from the room in a swirl of silver and deep blue. He nearly walked into the wall before he realized he was gawking at her again.

"I saw an article in the newspaper yesterday about an investment opportunity," Everett said, oblivious to Cord's fascination with his daughter. "I wanted to get your thoughts on it, Cord, seeing as how you're experienced with that sort of thing."

With one ear tuned to the kitchen, where the women's soft voices blended with the sounds of dishes clanking, Cord tried to give Everett his undivided attention. He took the newspaper article Everett held out to him, attempting to gather his wits.

"I don't know, sir. This looks like something shady to me," Cord said after he skimmed the article, then handed the paper back to the man. "You'd be better off investing in ..." Cord offered the names of several reputable companies, including one located in Heppner.

"Thanks, Cord. I knew I could count on you for sound advice."

Cord nodded to his host. "You're welcome. I'm always happy to help. If I'm not around, Luke is a good source too."

Everett wadded the article into a ball and tossed it into a basket by his desk. "True. I ran into your aunt this morning. She seems quite content now that she's remarried. I think she needed someone to fuss over."

"I agree. I know Luke and Filly worried they'd lose her too after Uncle Greg passed, but I'm so glad she's found happiness and purpose again with Mr. Rutherford. I wish them all the happiness their hearts can hold."

Everett thumped him on the shoulder. "I pray my Gracy will know that sort of affection someday." The older man gave Cord a searching look, then abruptly changed the subject to Tom Grove's family and something funny his daughter, Nina, had done when she and Lila had stopped by the newspaper office that afternoon. "I keep forgetting you and Lila are cousins. How many more relatives do you have that might someday show up in Hardman?"

"A few," Cord said, grinning at Everett.

"We're ready," Cleo announced as she and Gracy walked into the room. Gracy tipped her head, as though she was thoughtfully observing Cord, and it made him even more disconcerted than he'd already been.

"Then let's be on our way," Everett said in a cheerful tone, helping Cleo with her coat.

Cord stepped forward and took the black cape Gracy had started to reach for from the chair where she'd draped it earlier. He settled it around her shoulders, feeling relief that the shapeless garment would hide her delectable form. He took a deep breath, but her alluring scent pervaded his nose again and made him long to take a step closer, to breathe it in with abandon.

Fingers fumbling, Cord somehow managed to pull on his coat and follow the women outside as Everett closed the door.

"It's such a lovely night. Let's walk," Gracy suggested, her head tipped back to study the night sky.

It had yet to snow, but the temperatures had cooled off considerably during the day until it felt more like winter than autumn. However, it was only four blocks to the opera house, and none of them would likely freeze on the short journey.

"Excellent idea, darling," Cleo said, wrapping her arm around Everett's and cozying up to him as they started along the sidewalk.

Cord offered his arm to Gracy, but she looked at it as though he'd instead insulted her. She shoved her hands into a muff she carried and strolled behind her parents. Cord shortened his stride and fell into step beside her, but for the life of him, he couldn't think of a single intelligent thing to say.

Something about the feisty and sometimes infuriating woman left him feeling like a green boy, not a man who had loved and lost and was now raising a son on his own.

Bodie had been thrilled to have an invitation to play with his cousins at Granger House. The boy had chattered like an excited squirrel all the way into town. Cord was grateful to Luke and Filly for extending the invitation. Bodie spent far too little time with others his age, but when Cord sent him to school next year, he'd surely miss his son more than he could bear to consider.

"You look like you're trying to solve the problems of the world," Gracy said quietly as her parents conversed about fond memories of past holiday seasons in Hardman. "Something wrong?"

"No, Gracy. Nothing is wrong," Cord said, then released a long breath. "I was just thinking about how hard it will be to let Bodie go to school next year. The ranch will seem too quiet without him there."

"I'm sure it will be an adjustment for both of you, but Bodie seems like a child with a lively mind. He needs to have it challenged at school, and the teacher is excellent."

Cord glanced at her. "So I've heard. Luke's children love going to school. I thought about sending Bodie this year, but he's still so young, even if he is big for his age."

"Good evening tidings!" a group of passersby in a carriage shouted and waved as they headed for the opera house just up the street.

Cord hadn't paid any attention to their surroundings, focused instead on Gracy. Even swathed in the big cape, she was still far too lovely for his liking. He still hadn't completely decided if she was friend or foe, even though they'd agreed to be friends.

The way his thoughts tripped around her, like a three-legged mule on ice skates, he decided maybe he should just give up on thinking altogether. It might be far safer than trying to sort out his tangled feelings where Miss Gracy Randall was concerned.

Before he could do more than follow Everett and Cleo across the street, they arrived at the Hardman Opera House.

Solicitously, Cord stepped forward and held the door as Everett, Cleo, Gracy, and a few others who'd just arrived walked inside.

Warmth slapped Cord's cheeks as he moved into the lobby and stepped behind Gracy, helping her with her cape. He held his breath, lest her fragrance tantalize him again.

"I'll take our things to the coat room," Cord volunteered, gathering Everett's and Cleo's coats and hats, then moved to stand in the line at the coat room. After leaving their things there, Cord returned to the lobby to find Gracy laughing at something his cousin Ginny said.

Ginny looked like a younger version of her mother with her blonde hair, blue eyes, and fashionable attire. Her husband, Blake, stood behind her, looking like he'd rather be working with his horses or carving wood in his workshop than attending the event even though the man's family in England made him part of the titled set. If Cord wasn't mistaken, he thought Blake was a viscount and his father was an earl.

A hand thumped Cord on the back with such force, he took a quick step forward to catch himself. He glared at Luke. If Filly hadn't joined them, Cord may have given his cousin a sharp word or two.

"Filly, you look lovely as always. Remind me what it is you see in this ugly galoot you married," Cord teased, kissing the back of Filly's gloved hand.

"He may not be much to look at, but he's good for a laugh or two," Filly quipped, making Cord chuckle, while Luke slapped a hand to his chest in feigned indignation.

"Here now, wife. No need to be insulting," Luke said, glowering at Filly first and then Cord.

Everyone in town knew Luke and Filly Granger were madly in love and had been since they'd wed all those years ago on a chilly November day.

Filly wrapped her arm around Luke's and kissed his cheek, looking at him with love in her eyes and warmth in her smile. "You know I think you're the most handsome man in the whole county."

Luke sighed and turned toward Cord. "Well, that's depressing. She used to say I was the most handsome man in the whole world, then we made a trip to Pendleton last summer, and I've been demoted."

Cord raised an eyebrow and glanced at Filly. "What, or should I say whom, is so special in Pendleton?"

"They have two deputies there that are handsome beyond description," Ginny said, joining the conversation and winking at Cord.

"They weren't that good-looking," Blake said, scowling at his wife.

Ginny and Filly looked at each other, grinned, then nodded their heads.

Cleo and Everett laughed, and the conversation turned to the year's wheat harvest, cattle prices, and the upcoming skating party planned at Blake and Ginny's place.

"Perhaps if Luke doesn't cheat this year, I might win our annual race." Blake gave Luke a narrowed glare.

"I don't cheat, you're just a bad skater. Someone with two left feet really should stay off the ice," Luke taunted.

Cord worked to hide his grin, fully aware Blake and Luke were good friends in addition to being brothers-in-law. The two men took great pleasure in needling each other.

"Oh, it looks like it's time to take our seats," Cleo said as an usher made an announcement for everyone to be seated.

Despite her earlier prickly reaction to him, Cord cupped Gracy's elbow and guided her to their seats next to his cousins, in a row directly behind her parents.

After half an hour of sitting close to Gracy, breathing in her luscious fragrance, and spending more time watching the enchantment on her face than the musical troupe performing on the stage, he wondered when he'd lost his last lick of sense.

Surely, if he were in possession of even a dollop of any wisdom at all, he would have known asking Gracy to accompany him this evening would be a colossal mistake.

He still mourned Helen. Still missed her every day. Still blamed himself for not being there when she'd taken ill. If he had been, would she be alive? Would he still be living in Boston working in a banking job he'd come to realize he despised?

Cord did his best to swallow a sigh. As much as it had torn his heart apart to lose Helen and then his parents, Cord clung to the truth that God had a plan for his life even if he often struggled to remember he was not in control. His faith was the only thing that had kept him going on his darkest days of grief. On other days, it was Bodie who had pulled him back to reality. His son had needed him and continued to need him.

Doing his best to focus on the musicians onstage, Cord sank a little deeper into the plush theater seat and pondered what he needed from life. What he wanted. It had been a long time since he'd given it any consideration.

His father, like many of the Granger men, had gone into banking. It was expected that Cord would do the same. Even though he had a good head for business and did well in the job, he much preferred being a rancher. He knew Luke understood since his cousin spent only half his time working at the bank and the rest chasing after his cattle or one of his other pursuits.

Cord had needed to leave Boston to escape the memories that had threatened to suffocate him. He'd needed to turn his hand, along with his mind, to hard work, which is what he'd done with Juniper Creek Ranch. Between remodeling the house, painting and repairing all the outbuildings, adding the carriage house, making improvements to corrals and pasture fences, and building up the herd of cattle, he'd been too busy to think during the day and too exhausted at night to do more than fall into bed and sleep.

Then a fiery woman had shown up in his barn and left him feeling as though his life had shifted in a whole new direction.

In the time since Helen had been gone, Cord hadn't so much as given another woman a second glance. To him, it not only seemed like he'd be slighting Helen, but he also wasn't ready to think of anyone else but his wife.

Nevertheless, the arrival of Gracy Randall had certainly drawn his interest. He'd given her more glances than he could count. Their first awkward, rather irate meeting had proven she had a temper no one wanted to rile and a razor-sharp tongue that could cut him to the quick.

Since then, he'd observed she could be sweet, kind, and fun. She'd apologized multiple times for upsetting Bodie that day at the ranch. Honestly, Cord had no idea what had spurred his son's reaction to the woman when they'd gone to the Randalls' home when Bodie hadn't seemed upset about Gracy at the ranch.

Regardless, Bodie appeared to be warming up to her, and that was a good thing considering the high regard in which he and Bodie held Gracy's parents.

Cord had tried to block the vibrant woman from his thoughts, but it seemed impossible. In fact, that afternoon, he'd been working with a colt and let his thoughts wander so far off course, ruminating about the way Gracy's hair had looked tumbling around her shoulders, that the horse had landed a solid kick to his thigh, jerking him back to the present moment.

Absently, he rubbed the hoof-shaped bruise as he cast a covert glance at Gracy. Her eyes sparkled with joy, and she leaned slightly forward in her seat as one of the singers held an impressively high note. When she, along with the rest of the audience, began to clap, Cord joined in the applause, even though he had no idea what songs had been sung.

"Oh, that was marvelous!" Gracy said, turning to him with a radiant smile that made Cord long to kiss her rosy lips. Excitement pulsed from her, infecting him with her energy. "Thank you so much for inviting me. They really are as talented as I've heard."

"Wasn't that something, honey?" Cleo asked, turning to look back at them. "They all are incredibly talented, but the way Miss Langston held that last note ..." Cleo paused for effect. "Superb!"

"It was wonderful," Filly said from her seat on the other side of Gracy. "I'm so glad we were able to attend. When Kaelee woke up fussy this morning, I was sure we'd have to stay home, but she seemed perfectly fine the rest of the day. Maura wouldn't have been pleased if her baby sister cried the whole time we were gone."

"I sure appreciate Maura keeping an eye on Bodie for me," Cord said, smiling at his cousin's beautiful wife. With Filly's hair just a few shades darker than Gracy's, it made him question if the Granger men had a thing for redheaded women.

Then again, Helen had been dark-haired and brown-eyed. Bodie looked so much like his mama, sometimes it made Cord's chest tighten and ache just to see him. But he loved his son. Fiercely.

Despite the pain it sometimes inflicted, he was thankful every single day to have Bodie as a reminder of his beloved wife.

Filly placed a hand on his arm and offered him a gentle smile. "We are always so happy to have Bodie stay with us. He and Patrick have a grand time playing together. The things those two boys come up with. Do you know when Patrick broke his arm a few months ago, I found him and Bodie trying to beat off the cast with a hammer?"

Cord chuckled. "That sounds about right. Bodie can be a handful, but I'd rather have him that way than a child without any gumption."

"I agree," Luke said, settling his hands on his wife's shoulders. "Speaking of gumption, it's nice to see you still have some."

Cord glowered at Luke, hoping Gracy didn't catch on to what his cousin implied. He didn't need to ask to know Luke was referring to him asking Gracy to join him this evening.

Filly glanced at her husband over her shoulder. "Luke, we really should be going. I hate to leave Maura with all the children for too long." She looked at Cleo and Gracy. "Seth and Judd are there, along with Erin and Owen Dodd."

"At least Maura has Erin there to help her keep the children from burning the house down. They both likely had their work cut out for them, though," Cleo said, grinning at Filly, then at Cord. "Would you like to come back to the house for dessert? I made chocolate pudding."

"If he doesn't want to come, I will," Luke joked, earning a glare from both Filly and Cleo.

Cord glowered at Luke, then smiled at Cleo. "I'd like that, Cleo. Thank you for asking."

"Patrick would be so happy if you allowed Bodie to spend the night. What do you say?" Luke asked as their group headed toward the door.

"I don't know, Luke." Cord was hesitant to agree, just because he wasn't sure he liked the idea of Bodie being anywhere but with him at night. "It might be best to take him home."

Filly placed her hand on his arm again and gave him such a pleading look, he couldn't muster the will to tell her no. He wondered how Luke got anything accomplished with such a pretty, sweet wife.

"Please, Cord? Patrick would be thrilled, and keeping Bodie overnight is no trouble at all. We could bring him home in the morning," Filly offered.

"I've been meaning to come out and see that colt you've been working with," Luke said. "Bringing Bodie home will give me an excuse to come out to your place."

"Sounds to me like it's all settled," Ginny said, winking at Cord as she and Blake entered the conversation.

Cord retrieved their coats and held the cape while Gracy slipped it on. He thought about holding his breath so her fragrance had no more opportunity to ensnare his overwrought senses, but he couldn't keep from breathing it in any more than he could refuse the need for air in his lungs.

What was happening to him?

In the short time since he'd met the woman, she'd somehow gotten under his skin and he didn't want her there. Or did he? No. He'd married the love of his life and she'd died far too young. He would be content on the ranch, just him and Bodie.

At least he attempted to convince himself of that as he and Gracy strolled under a blanket of stars. Everett and Cleo had accepted a ride from friends who would drop them off at the house.

"I don't know when I've seen such a lovely night," Gracy mused as she tipped back her head and stared up at the sky.

Stars glittered in her magnificent eyes, making them seem luminous in the moonlight. Cord couldn't help but compare the night sky to the beautiful gown she wore. His hands had itched all evening to touch that soft velvet. Would it feel as warm beneath his fingers as he imagined?

"I don't know when I've seen such a lovely gown as the one you're wearing tonight," Cord said in a low, husky voice. "You are a beautiful woman, Gracy Randall."

He was sure if it hadn't been dark out, he'd have been able to see the bright pink of a blush stain both of her cheeks as she turned her head to look at him as though gauging his sincerity. She must have been satisfied with what she saw in his expression and eyes.

Her smile softened, then she turned her attention back to the sky. "You're fairly handsome, Mr. Granger. I had no idea you could clean up so well. Are those some of your banker clothes? Mama mentioned you used to be an investment banker."

He glanced down at the suit he wore, the polished shoes, and the hat that was the last thing a cowboy might wear. "Yes. I kept a few suits, but I'd much rather wear jeans and boots."

"They do seem to *suit* you," she said with a teasing grin.

He smiled, and the tension between them melted away. "How did job hunting go this week?"

"Good, and not well," she said, grasping his arm as she stepped on an icy spot and slid on the slick surface.

Cord pulled his arm close against his side and tightened the muscles to give her a more solid surface to grip as she caught her balance, and they continued walking. Much to his surprise, she didn't relinquish her hold on his arm.

"What does that mean?" he asked, wondering what she'd do if he held her hand, or did something as bold as kiss her cheek. Why now, after almost two years of not giving another woman even a passing thought, had his attention been so thoroughly captured by Gracy?

"The mercantile wasn't hiring, but I did spend two days helping Aleta with her holiday displays. George even sent me out on a few deliveries. Filly offered to pay me with the same tip she always gave Percy. Apparently, a handful of warm cookies were preferred to cash when he was a boy."

Cord chuckled. "Considering Filly's cookies, I could see why. If his parents enlist his help, Percy might still accept that as payment."

"Filly is a fantastic cook, isn't she? Not that my mother's cooking lacks anything, but Filly's is just extra delicious."

Their discussion of delicious things nudged his thoughts to how delicious he was sure Gracy's mouth would taste. Ashamed of himself, Cord redirected his runaway thoughts. "So, you helped Aleta for two days. Then what did you do?"

"Brynn hired me to help her with her holiday displays. Percy won't be back until Tuesday evening, and she didn't want to wait for his return to decorate the shop. We spent part of the morning crawling around in the attic looking for a box of decorations that took forever to find. It was fun to help her, though, and I enjoyed getting to know her better. We knew each other in school, but it was nice to chat with her as adults."

"I imagine it's a change to come home all grown up and see things in a different light," Cord said. Would things in Boston look far different if he ever decided to return there for a visit? He'd been born and raised there and couldn't imagine never setting foot in the town again.

"It is different but in a good way," Gracy said, stopping as they waited for two buggies and an auto to pass before they crossed the street. "I've asked all around town, but no one seems to be in need of help, which is odd, considering it is the holiday season and a busy time of year for most of the shops and businesses."

"That does seem strange. I did happen to notice a help wanted sign in the skating rink window when I passed by yesterday. I don't have any idea what type of work it might be, but you might check there."

"I'll do that. Thank you, Cord." She gave him a long glance as they turned at the corner and headed toward her parents' house down the block. "Also, thank you for this evening. It's been one of the nicest evenings I've had in a long, long time."

"It's been my pleasure to escort you, Gracy." There was so much he wanted to say, but he refrained as they hurried up the steps and inside the Randall home.

After enjoying cups of coffee and the pudding Cleo had made earlier, Cord knew he needed to head home.

"Thank you for another wonderful meal, Cleo, and for the pudding. It hit the spot after our entertaining evening." Cord stood and carried his coffee cup and pudding dish to the sink. "I really should get home, though."

"We're so glad you could join us this evening," Cleo said, giving him a hug, then stepping back so he could shake hands with Everett. He tried not to grin when he saw Cleo elbow Gracy in the side, as though prompting her forward.

Gracy gave her mother a quashing glance, then turned to him. "I'll walk you out, Cord."

"Thanks again. I'll see you Sunday at church."

"We'll be there," Everett said, wrapping a hand around Cleo's waist and pulling her back against him.

Cord could feel them watching as he and Gracy headed to the front door, where he'd left his hat and coat. He shrugged into the coat, picked up the hat, and opened the door. To his surprise, Gracy followed him outside, quietly pulling the door shut behind her.

"I do thank you, Cord, for such a pleasant evening. It's one I'll long remember." Gracy held her hands clasped behind her back as they slowly walked down the porch steps.

Cord was sure she had no idea how the pose thrust her chest forward and drew his attention to it. The moon shone on her like a spotlight, dancing with the silver threads of her gown and setting them to sparkling like diamonds floating at sea.

Mesmerized, Cord felt like time slowed until it stood still. With effort, he dragged his gaze to Gracy's face and found her smiling at him.

"I'm glad you had a nice time, Gracy. I did too. Perhaps we could do something like this again."

"I'd like that very much, Cord. Thank you." She glanced up at the sky, then shivered. "It's starting to feel more like winter."

"It is." He took a step closer to her, then another, removing the space that had lingered between them. He wanted to pull her to his chest. To hold her tight. To kiss those delectable lips and satisfy his longing to know if they tasted as decadent as he imagined.

"You are a wonder of a woman, Gracy." Instead of giving in to his yearning to kiss her, to love her, he brushed his thumb over the curve of her cheek, reveling in the silky feel of her skin. "I'll see you soon."

Before he could change his mind, before he did something he was sure he'd regret, he raced down the walk and out to his auto that he'd left parked in front of the house. With a final wave at Gracy, he drove down the street, fighting with himself over his conflicting feelings.

On the cold drive home, he realized what he wanted—what he desperately wanted—was Gracy Randall.

The fact that he did left him unable to sleep, tossing and turning long into the night once he settled into his bed. Nothing good could come from his interest in the woman. Not when Cord was certain his heart still belonged to his wife.

Chapter Seven

Cord had barely slept and woke early, still feeling unsettled and unlike himself. He chided himself for letting thoughts of Gracy Randall rob him of his sleep and peace.

After drinking two cups of coffee strong enough to strip the silver off his spoon, and slapping a hunk of leftover ham between two slices of bread, he stepped outside and breathed in the crisp morning breeze.

Plumes of steam from the coffee cup he held rose in the frosty air. It wouldn't be long until snow coated the ground. There was an abundance of work to see to before then. He just needed to focus on it instead of one enchanting redheaded woman who'd recently stormed into his life.

He looked at the big stack of wood that he'd hauled home a few weeks ago. It needed to be chopped into firewood and stacked against the back porch, ready to use during the winter months.

Cord chewed the last bite of his breakfast, drained the coffee cup, and set it inside the kitchen sink, then returned outside, ready to tackle the firewood.

Five minutes after he started chopping wood, he shed his coat, tossing it over the back porch railing out of the way along with his hat. The exertion felt good, and he lost himself in the task.

He recalled how close he'd come to kissing Gracy last night as he'd stood on the front walk with her in the moonlight. His lips still tingled for the want of her kiss every time he thought about how beautiful she'd looked bathed in the silvery light.

Part of him felt like he betrayed Helen by feeling anything for anyone. He'd vowed to love her his whole life, and he knew he would. But a more rational part of his brain reminded him the vows that he'd made were until death parted him and Helen.

He contemplated what it would be like to love a woman like Gracy Randall. She was nothing like his wife. Not a thing.

Helen had always been quiet and reserved, a little on the timid side, but caring and giving. He'd fallen in love with her so easily because they'd grown up as neighbors and friends. One day, he'd glanced at her as he'd spoken with the pastor after church and realized Helen had grown up. The next day, he'd asked to court her, and two months later, they'd wed.

Everything with Helen had always been so affable. They'd rarely argued or disagreed. Helen had run their home with quiet efficiency. At the end of a long day, Cord had counted on returning to an immaculate house, a soft-spoken wife, and a filling meal. Now, though, he wondered if there were times Helen would have liked to speak her mind or differ from his opinion. He'd recently realized she'd always relinquished her wishes to align with his.

That wasn't what he'd wanted or even expected, but somehow that's the way their marriage had gone, and he'd been too busy to even notice. Helen had lived in his shadow, and he hadn't been even vaguely aware of it until after she'd passed and he'd finally forced himself to examine their relationship. One of the rare times they'd argued was about the last trip he'd taken when she'd fallen ill. He recalled she'd been pale the morning he'd left, and she'd begged him not to go. He'd assured her it was a quick three-day trip and he'd be back before she could miss him.

He'd been so selfish and cocky and sure of himself, he'd never once stopped to think that Helen might have needed him. Too soon, she was gone.

It didn't help to dwell on the what ifs of his life, though. All that accomplished was to give him a roaring headache, and he wasn't in the mood to get sucked into dark thoughts of his past today.

The loud whine of a motorcycle disturbed the peaceful morning, drawing Cord back to the moment. He buried the blade of the axe in a thick stump, wiped the sweat from his forehead on a kerchief he took from his back pocket, then stretched his back.

By the position of the sun, he'd been chopping wood far longer than he'd planned. He hadn't set out with the intention of cutting such a large pile, but the physical exertion felt good and gave his scattered thoughts time to roam.

Cord tucked the kerchief back in his pocket and walked around to the front yard. He watched as Luke sped up the lane and slid to a stop a few feet away from Cord as he reached the edge of the yard.

"I'm sure glad to see Bodie isn't riding that thing with you," Cord chastised his cousin. "If he were, I'd feel obliged to knock some sense into you for endangering my son."

Luke scowled as he removed a pair of goggles and dangled them from the handlebars of his motorcycle. "I'm not nearly as dumb as you and my wife seem to think I am. Just this morning, Filly warned me, twice, about not giving the children rides. It's not like I haven't heard that same warning every time I ride this fine machine." Luke patted the side of the motorcycle as though it was his favorite horse.

"What brings you out to the ranch without Bodie?" Cord tugged off his gloves and smacked them against his thigh, then winced when he hit the bruise the colt had given him.

"The kids are having such a high ol' time playing together, they begged for Bodie to stay one more night. If you're agreeable, I can take some clothes in for him to change into tomorrow for church. We'll give him back to you after the service."

"Are you sure he's no trouble?" Cord asked, taking a step toward the back door while Luke rolled the motorcycle onto the kickstand. "I know he can be a rascal."

"He's no more trouble than my little hooligans. Between Cullen and Patrick, Maura is already counting the days until she's old enough to leave home, although I have no idea what she intends to do. That girl is far too interested in boys and romance for my liking."

Cord chuckled as he held open the back door and Luke preceded him inside. "Isn't that what most sixteen-year-old girls are focused on? Boys, clothes, and romance. Maybe even in that order."

"Oh, the order changes from hour to hour, but those are the three main topics she enjoys discussing, at least with Erin Dodd and occasionally her mother. Anytime I ask a question, she rolls her eyes and gives me that same you're-an-idiot look I get from Filly when I ask her for a second helping of dessert."

"I've seen you around pumpkin pie," Cord teased, brushing the bits of wood and bark off his pants and shirt before he stepped inside. "You just wait until you think everyone is asleep and sneak down to the kitchen to help yourself to a third serving."

SHANNA HATFIELD

Luke slapped him on the shoulder. "And you only know that because you were already in the kitchen devouring your second—or was it third?—slice of coconut cake."

Cord shrugged and turned on the faucet to wash his hands at the kitchen sink. "I'd offer to have you stay for lunch, but I'm no better at cooking than Ginny."

A chuckle rolled out of Luke. "It's a good thing Blake didn't marry her for her cooking or cleaning skills. He knew what he was getting before he proposed."

Cord nodded and moved out of the way so Luke could wash his hands. "It's nice to see them so happy together. And Aunt Dora practically glows with joy. I'm glad she married Mr. Rutherford after you lost your dad."

"I'm glad she did too. He's a good man, and Mother is plumb daffy over him." Luke offered Cord a sly grin as he finished washing his hands. "Speaking of being daffy, you were sure making eyes at Gracy Randall last night. They could have turned off all the lights in the theater and let the sparks shooting between you two illuminate the whole place. What's going on?"

"Nothing," Cord growled, wondering when his cousin had gotten so perceptive. Maybe it was from having a daughter who was nearly grown.

Luke bumped him with his elbow. "Come on. You can talk to me, Cord. I'm always happy to impart my years of hard-earned wisdom."

Cord snorted. "You do like to palaver on and on and on, cousin."

"You know," Luke leaned back against the counter as he dried his hands on a towel, "for a man who's just been given the gift of a child-free Saturday, you might want to be a little nicer to me."

Cord held his hands up in front of him in a placating motion, then picked up the coffee pot from the stove. Enough remained to partially fill two cups. He poured the coffee and handed one to Luke, then motioned to the small kitchen table.

"I recognize that look on your face. It's a mixture of confusion, determination, and stubbornness with a dash of lovesickness mixed in," Luke observed, taking a seat in a chair across from Cord. "How long have you been sweet on Gracy?"

"Considering I've barely known her a full week, I can't say what I am, exactly. I haven't even fully decided I like the woman. Our first meeting didn't go well. I told you about her showing up expecting to find her folks here and being as angry as a bee-stung bear."

"You did mention that," Luke said, taking a sip of the coffee. "What happened between then and last night?"

"I'm not sure," Cord sighed. "All I know is every time I think about her, I …well, I think I'd like to get to know her better, but then I get lost in memories of Helen and I'm not sure I should pursue anything with anyone."

Luke nodded. "I can't even begin to imagine how hard this has been for you, losing your wife, then your folks. If I lost Filly, I don't know how I'd go on, but Chauncy would remind me that God has plans I can't begin to understand, and my job is just to walk one faithful step at a time."

"Pastor Dodd does share some rather poignant nuggets of wisdom." Cord knew Luke and Chauncy Dodd had been best friends for decades. The pastor's wife, Abby, was one of Filly's dearest friends, and their daughter, Erin, was Maura's closest friend.

"Don't mention that to Chauncy. You might give him a big head," Luke teased, then his expression turned solemn. "I don't know what advice to give you, Cord, other than to follow your heart. Our heads sometimes have a habit of getting in the way of our happiness. Do what your heart tells you to do, and you'll likely stay on track. I didn't know your Helen well, but I do know she wanted, above all else, for you to be happy. I don't think she'd expect you to remain alone forever, and I'm certain she'd want Bodie to grow up knowing a mother's love."

Cord rubbed his hand along the back of his neck. "That's another problem. The first time she was here, Gracy got upset with Bodie and yelled at him. He wasn't hurting anything that mattered to me. You know how bad the flies were during that warm spell we had. Bodie took great delight in smacking them with a mallet that had belonged to Gracy's grandfather. When she saw him beating first the hitching post and then the stepping stones with it, she lost her temper. Honestly, I think it was more about discovering the ranch was no longer in her family than anything Bodie did. That evening, when we went to Everett and Cleo's place for dinner, Bodie started screaming and crying the moment she opened the door, ranting about the mean, scary lady."

Luke chuckled. "I'm sure that made for an awkward meal."

"It did, and to Gracy's credit, she apologized multiple times, and has tried to make amends with Bodie. He doesn't seem to be in any hurry to forgive her for her transgressions, although he did seem to enjoy it when she asked him to help her play the piano. I don't know if I should stay away from her solely on the fact that Bodie hasn't decided if he will eventually come around to liking her."

"He's resilient and smart, and I think he doesn't dislike her as much as he might have led you to believe. I heard him telling Patrick about the pretty lady with her hair on fire who plays the piano. He was raving about how she smelled nice and let him play her piano whenever he wanted."

"Well, how about that. I'll give it some more thought, but for now, I'd appreciate it if you'd not mention our conversation to anyone." Cord released a long breath. "I reckon I have some thoughts to sort through and should do that before I consider pursuing Gracy."

"That's a smart plan, cousin. Just don't drag your feet too long. A beautiful woman like her won't stay single for long."

Cord felt like pointing out that she'd remained single the whole time she'd lived in Grass Valley but kept his thoughts to himself. Instead, he noticed Luke looking around the kitchen.

"You still thinking about hiring a housekeeper and cook?" Luke asked.

"Yep. It's something I need to get taken care of, but finding just the right person is far down on my list of tasks."

"I'll ask Filly and Ginny if they know anyone who might be good. Ginny won't share Mrs. Cole with anyone, and our housekeeper only works part-time as it is, but they might have some ideas."

Cord nodded. "I'm not in a rush, Luke. I was figuring on looking for someone after the holidays. However, it would sure be nice to come in from a day of work and have the house smelling like Christmas instead of the previous night's overcooked beans or stew."

Luke laughed. "I know exactly what you mean. Before I married Filly, I had no idea how much I needed her in my life. Now, I can't begin to picture what a day without her would look like."

"It's wonderful, and encouraging, to see the two of you still so deeply in love even after all these years. I've noticed there are several couples like that in town. Why even Arlan Guthry can hardly keep his numbers straight when his wife walks by the bank."

"Don't I know it. Alex isn't just a prestidigitator; she's cast some sort of magical spell over Arlan."

Cord chuckled. "I wondered how long it would take you to work that word into the conversation. According to Blake, you use it any chance you can."

"Blake is full of hot air and horse feathers half the time," Luke groused, scowling as he rose and set his empty coffee cup in the sink. "Speaking of my brother-in-law, with the warm weather we've had and the lack of snow, he's sure he'll have to cancel the annual skating party at his place."

"That's too bad. I've heard so many in town talk about it with excitement. Could they hold a party anyway, even without the skating? Maybe there could be some races or games."

Luke perked up at the mention of races. "Now you're talking. I'll run by Blake's place on my way home and see what he has to say."

Cord shook his head. "You do know Blake's place is clear on the other side of town about four miles from here."

Luke grinned. "I'm aware of the location, but it gives me an excuse to spend more time riding my motorcycle. Once it snows, I won't get to use it again until the mud dries up in the spring."

"It's a wonder you don't break your neck on that thing." Cord pointed to a tin on the counter. "Cleo left some cookies for me the other day. Help yourself while I gather Bodie's things."

Cord hurried upstairs and got two changes of clothes for his son, knowing Bodie could very well spill something all over himself right before church. He tucked the clothes into a little bag, added the boy's favorite storybook, then took a moment to look around his son's room. Despite Bodie's lively tendencies, he liked his room to be neat and orderly, which always struck Cord as odd.

If left to his own devices for more than ten minutes, Bodie could whip through the house like a tornado, but his bedroom would remain tidy. It wasn't a bad trait to have. Perhaps, in time, he could get the boy to be a little more helpful in keeping the rest of the house picked up too.

Cord jogged downstairs, thinking Bodie got his fastidiousness from Helen. She'd always liked things just so, but she'd never complained when Cord had kicked off his boots in one corner and left his pants in another. She'd just quietly picked them up and restored order.

A pang of regret hit him for all the times he'd caused her extra work that was unnecessary. He should have been more thoughtful, more caring, more loving toward his tender-hearted wife.

Unwilling to let his maudlin thoughts overtake him again, he found Luke out by the corral, looking at the colt and giving the dogs some extra attention. They'd gone off with the ranch hands earlier to check the fence lines, but it appeared they'd returned, most likely ready for a midday meal.

Cord wouldn't mind something to eat either, but it meant he'd either have to find something to cook or go into town to eat. He decided to wander over to the bunkhouse and give Luke's suggestion of hiring a housekeeper and cook more consideration.

"If you change your mind, just telephone and I'll come get Bodie," Cord said, leaning an arm against the fence.

"He'll be fine. We'll see you at church. If you don't have any better offers, the two of you are welcome to join us for lunch after the service."

"Thanks, Luke. I don't have any plans in place just yet."

Luke smirked at him. "But I bet you're hoping Cleo extends an invitation to join them. Can't blame you a bit."

Cord started to protest, then thought better of it. He *was* hoping Cleo would invite him and Bodie for lunch, as she had many of the past Sundays. He usually took something like boxed chocolates or a treat from the bakery to share. He also intended to give Cleo and Everett half a beef when he butchered next week as a thank you to them for all they'd done to help him since he'd arrived in Hardman.

"The colt looks like a fine one," Luke said as they walked back to where he'd left his motorcycle.

"I hope he'll turn out to be a good mount." Cord watched as Luke pulled on his goggles and started the motorcycle.

"Enjoy a quiet day to yourself," Luke said, taking the bag of Bodie's things that Cord held out to him.

"You too!" Cord shouted above the roar of the machine, then waved as Luke raced down the lane toward the road.

Cord went back to chopping wood. It seemed like as good a place as any to sort through his tangled thoughts.

Chapter Eight

"Thank you for the opportunity," Gracy said, politely nodding to the owner of the town's roller skating rink. Normally, it wasn't busy in the winter since there were many places to ice skate, but since it had yet to snow and had only begun to freeze, business still appeared to be booming.

Gracy had been grateful to Cord for telling her he'd seen a *help wanted* sign in the window of the business. She'd gone there first thing Saturday morning and been hired on the spot.

"You'll do fine, Miss Randall. It's simple, really. Just rent out the skates, make sure no one tears up the rink, and put the skates away. At the end of the day, count the money and place it and a receipt in the box I showed you beneath the counter, then turn out the lights and lock the doors, and that's all there is to it." Mr. Gardner took a key ring from his pocket, removed a key, and handed it to her. "Any questions?"

"How much do I charge?" she asked.

Mr. Gardner showed her a plaque on the front counter with the prices, where all the skates were kept, and where she could find cleaning supplies if she needed them.

"If you don't burn the place down today, I'll look forward to seeing you back here on Monday."

Before she could voice another question, Mr. Gardner disappeared out the door, leaving Gracy alone. She removed her hat but left on her coat since it was chilly inside the big building.

She'd barely taken a seat at the desk behind the counter when the bell above the door jangled and the first customers of the day strode in. From that point on, the minutes blurred into hours. Gracy felt like she'd been caught in a whirlwind. It seemed half the population of Hardman had decided to come skating that day. Just trying to make sure everyone rented skates that fit was enough to keep her hopping from one customer to the next.

Her mother dropped by and saw she was busy, waggling her fingers and giving her an encouraging smile before she raced back out the door. If she'd lingered, Gracy might have begged her mother for help.

A group of three boys got into a fight in the middle of the rink, and Gracy had to work her way out to them to break it up. Two of them, engaged in fisticuffs, ended up inadvertently hitting her when the third member of their group pushed them toward her. She fell in a heap of petticoats and skirts on the floor of the rink, but she managed to keep her temper from boiling over, barely. She did escort the boys out of the rink and hovered over them as they removed the skates, then ordered them out of the building before they caused more trouble.

While she was fussing with them, customers had lined up to rent skates and she had a terrible time trying to keep up with them and those returning skates.

One little scamp lost his lunch all over the floor, which caused a horrific chain reaction that Gracy was left to clean up. It was only by keeping her nose turned into her shoulder and taking shallow breaths that she managed the task. That, and her stomach was as empty as a forgotten post hole, as the ranch foreman used to say since she'd left the house without breakfast and had no way of procuring lunch.

By mid-afternoon, she was dirty, tired, bruised, hungry, and wondering if the few coins Mr. Gardner had agreed to pay her for the day were worth the bother.

When another group of unruly youngsters came in and started shoving each other, yelling like wild beasts, Gracy concluded it was not.

Two boys got in a fight over a girl, ending when one punched the other in the nose and blood spurted everywhere, including on the girl. She raced out of the rink, crying, and tossed her skates at Gracy, hitting her on the cheek with one on her way out the door. Gracy went to get the boys off the skating rink floor. As thanks for her trouble, the boy with the bloody nose managed to drip all over her coat.

Gracy wanted to scream in frustration, but she didn't. She cleaned up the blood and suggested the boy head to the doctor's office, then prayed for the strength to last until closing time.

It seemed like she'd been trapped at the rink for years, not hours, when she glanced at the clock and saw it was finally time to close for the evening. After counting the money and leaving it with a receipt in the box Mr. Gardner had shown her, she made sure all the skates were put away, tidied the desk and the rest of the building, then stepped outside with a relieved sigh.

Her breath turned into frosty feathers that floated upward as she walked home, deciding she would rather scrub floors as a scullery maid than work another day at the skating rink.

"Is that you, honey?" her mother called as Gracy entered her parents' home through the front door, too tired to troop around to the kitchen door.

"It's me, Mama," Gracy shrugged out of her filthy coat, removed her hat and gloves, and left them hanging on hooks by the door before she wearily walked to the kitchen.

"I made chicken with—" Cleo's words trailed off and her eyes widened as she took in Gracy's disheveled state. "My lands, honey! What on earth happened to you? Is that a bruise on your cheek?"

Gracy's fingers touched the tender skin where the girl had unwittingly hit her with a skate.

"Probably. I can't go back there, Mama. It was terrible. Worse than terrible. It was a nightmare. Boys got into fights, and one bled all over my coat. One little boy threw up and suddenly there was a river of ..."

Cleo held up a hand to stop her from saying more. "You don't need to go into detail, darling. I can smell what happened on you. Go take a bath. A nice, long hot one. It will make you feel better. I'll bring you something to wear. By the time you're clean, I'll have supper on the table."

Gracy was too tired to argue when her mother gave her a shove toward the bathroom door. As water filled the tub, she removed her filthy clothes. After kicking them into the hallway, Gracy slowly sank into the hot water and felt herself relax for the first time all day. She scrubbed her skin twice with her favorite floral soap, then washed her hair. When she got out to dry, she noticed the bruises on her legs and arms from being run into and over and falling onto the floor of the rink.

Mind made up, she would return the key to Mr. Gardner Monday morning and inform him he should put the *help wanted* sign back in the window because there was nothing that would compel her to spend another day working there.

Rather than be dismayed about being once again unemployed, Gracy felt relief at having survived such a trying day. She fluffed her curls with her fingers, dressed in the clothes her mother had slipped into the room, then hurried to the kitchen.

She found her parents dancing across the kitchen while her father hummed a tune. Gracy leaned against the doorway and watched them. A smile broke across her lips when her mother started to sing about not being allowed to see a boy, but he came and took her for a walk along a snowy lane.

When her father spun her mother around, they both noticed Gracy.

"Oh, darling, there you are. Supper is ready," her mother said, looking slightly embarrassed as her cheeks turned pink.

"That was a cute song, Mama. Is it an old one?" Gracy asked as she moved into the room and began helping dish up the meal.

"Yes. It's one I used to sing when your father and I were courting. Your grandfather didn't approve of him. Thought he was wild and worthless. I was forbidden to see him, but Everett would walk over after the evening chores were through, and we'd take a stroll in the moonlight. We never stayed out too long for fear of getting caught, but I treasured each moment of those special times."

Gracy saw the loving looks her parents exchanged and knew she wanted that in her own life. She wanted to be loved so deeply and completely by another. Someday, she hoped to know that kind of deep, abiding affection that lasted for more than fifty years.

"How did you convince Grandpa to let Papa court you?" Gracy asked as she filled glasses with milk and set them on the table.

"Your father asked to speak to him one afternoon after church. He wanted to take me for a sleigh ride." Cleo took a seat in the chair Everett held for her, then glanced at him over her shoulder with a tender smile. "Everett never would tell me exactly what was said, but after that, I was allowed to court him, and we wed three months later."

"Then ten years later you had Rob." Gracy hadn't realized she'd spoken aloud until she looked up to see the pain on her parents' faces. "I'm sorry," she said, ducking her head.

"No, honey, it's fine." Cleo reached out and squeezed her hand reassuringly. "The grief will never go away, but from time to time, it's good to talk about those we love who are no longer with us. We'll always miss Rob, Julie, and the children, just like you'll always miss Samuel. But they'll always be in our hearts."

Gracy nodded, feeling the sting of tears burning her eyes, but she blinked them away.

"We lost four babies before Rob was born and three more before we had you," Cleo said, gently pushing a wayward curl behind Gracy's ear. "You and Rob were the most precious gifts we've ever received."

Gracy had no idea her parents had lost seven babies. A hundred questions flew through her thoughts, but now wasn't the time to voice them. "We couldn't have asked for better parents than the two of you."

Everett leaned forward and kissed Gracy's forehead, then settled back in his chair, held out his hands, and offered a heartfelt word of thanks for their meal and asked a special blessing on anyone who was grieving that evening.

As food was passed around the table, Gracy saw her parents in a new light. One rimmed with more loss and heartache than she could even imagine.

Her father asked about her day, and she made him laugh, talking about all the craziness of trying to manage the skating rink.

"I heard the restaurant is hiring," Everett said, giving his daughter a long glance. "It can't be worse than what you put up with today."

"It certainly can't. How hard can it be to take orders and bring people their food?" Gracy asked, grinning at her father.

Tuesday evening, after she'd spent all day on her feet rushing from table to table, taking orders, delivering food, filling water glasses, pouring cups of coffee, and evading the groping hands of one ill-mannered salesman who'd wandered in off the afternoon stage, Gracy decided she might prefer the skating rink to working at a restaurant.

It had been so fast-paced and hectic, she hadn't been able to take a break let alone eat lunch. Her feet screamed in protest each time she took a step. Despite the voluminous white apron she wore, her shirtwaist and skirt were stained with food and spills, and her hands were raw and red from plunging them into scalding dishwater when she'd been pressed into service helping wash dishes after the lunch crowd had dispersed.

Her hair hung in straggling strands around her face, and she knew she looked like she'd ridden backward on a twister. The only thing keeping her going was the thought of going home and soaking in a tub of hot water, then collapsing in her soft, warm bed.

She glanced outside and saw snowflakes had begun to fall.

"Looks like it might be a white Christmas after all," one of the old-timers mused as he shuffled toward the door.

"That would be nice, wouldn't it, Mr. Hughes?" Gracy said, handing him his coat from the rack by the door after he paid for his meal.

"I'm not so fond of the cold and snow, but it does make the season seem more special. You suppose Blake and Ginny Stratton will be able to have their skating party?"

Gracy shrugged. "I don't know, sir, but I heard even if there's no skating, they plan to have a party just the same."

"Well, that's good. It's become quite a tradition to head out there for a day of fun. I remember the year Blake and Luke ..." the older gent recalled several funny stories of things Blake and Luke had done while Gracy practically danced off one foot to another. Finally, Mr. Hughes pulled on a pair of bright red mittens, tipped his head to her, and sauntered out the door.

Gracy rushed to wait on three more customers, made a hasty trip to the necessary out back, grateful all over again for indoor plumbing in her parents' home, and returned inside stamping the snow from her shoes and blowing on her icy fingers.

"Gracy, take those two orders out, would you?" The chef raised his voice to be heard over the racket in the kitchen and placed three plates into her hands.

With her shoes wet from the snow, Gracy took one step and slid across the floor, colliding with another waitress. The plates they held shot upward, then crashed to the floor with a raucous noise as plates broke and silverware clanged. Gracy slipped and fell on top of the mess, dragging down poor Miss Langley with her.

The cacophony in the kitchen and the dining area settled into silence until the only sound was of a china saucer spinning around on its rim.

"Out! Get out of my kitchen!" the chef yelled, shaking a spoon dripping with gravy at Gracy. "I'd be better off with trained monkeys working in here than you, Miss Randall. Out!"

Mortified, Gracy tried to get up, but her feet continued to slip beneath her on the food-covered floor. A beefy hand reached down and hauled her upright. The chef shoved money into her hand and pushed her toward the door.

"Do not come back. Not ever!" he hollered.

Gracy whipped off the apron, tossed it on a hook by the door, grabbed her coat, and fled into the snowy night.

She refused to pull on her recently cleaned coat over her clothes that were dripping everything from country gravy to smashed squash. Instead, she ran toward her parents' home, wondering how she could have lost another job already. Perhaps she should just pack her bags and leave before she disgraced her family. Surely, news would travel around town about her flitting from one job to the next, and soon no one would give her a chance.

The accident at the restaurant wasn't entirely her fault. If she hadn't been so tired, and weak from hunger, and her shoes hadn't been damp from the snow, she wouldn't have slipped into Miss Langley and wasted all that food, or broken the dishes.

Gracy took the back steps two at a time and plowed inside the house. She tossed her coat over a hook at the back door and rubbed her hands over her arms as her nose and cheeks tingled from the warmth.

Shivers rolled over her, and she hoped she wouldn't catch some grave malady from racing through town in the snow with damp clothes and no coat.

"Oh, my heavens!" Cleo shrieked when she stepped into the hallway from the front room.

"What is it?" Everett asked, hurrying to stand behind her.

Gracy met her father's gaze, and the two of them burst out laughing.

"I don't see what is humorous at all," Cleo snapped, rushing into the bathroom to fill the tub with hot water. "She'll catch her death. Just look at her. Gracy's teeth are chattering, and she's shivering like she's been locked in an icehouse."

Her father stepped in front of Gracy and took her hands in his, rubbing warmth into her frigid fingers. "Might we assume you won't be returning to the restaurant?"

"That would be an accurate assumption, Papa. I'm not sure the chef will even allow me to eat there again."

Cleo raised her nose in the air. "His food isn't as good as mine anyway."

"No, it isn't," Gracy agreed, winking at her father. "My shoes were wet. I slipped on the floor and crashed into Miss Langley, and we ended up in a pile of broken dishes and ruined food. The chef made it perfectly clear I'm not to return."

"That's his loss, honey," Everett said, starting to kiss her forehead, then pulling back.

Gracy reached up and wiped away a glob of butter, then broke into giggles.

"I think she's losing her grasp on reality, Everett!" Cleo's voice held concern as she spoke from the bathroom. "Bring her in here so I can get her in the tub."

"I'm fine, Mama, but thank you for drawing the bath for me. I didn't get a chance to eat all day. I don't suppose you have something I could nibble on once I get all this scrubbed off me?" Gracy asked, sweeping a hand over her ruined shirtwaist and skirt.

"Of course, darling. You clean up and I'll get something ready for you."

"Thanks, Mama," Gracy smiled at her mother and waited until the woman closed the bathroom door to step out of her filthy clothes and then sink into the tub. Exhausted, but starving, Gracy scrubbed her skin, washed her hair, and dressed in the soft flannel gown and robe her mother had brought in for her to wear. She tugged warm knitted slippers on her feet, combed the tangles from her hair, tightened the belt of her robe, then hurried to the kitchen.

Her mother gave her a cup of tea, then lifted a tray. "Let's get you in by the fire, Gracy. No need to sit here in the kitchen."

"Thank you," Gracy said, following her mother down the hall to the front room, where her father stoked the fire into a merry blaze that filled the room with welcome heat. "Oh, that feels good." Gracy stood with her back to the fireplace, letting the warmth seep into her. Despite her bath, she still felt chilled. She sipped from the cup of spicy, sweetened tea and let it glide down her throat. "That tastes wonderful, Mama."

"I'm glad you like it, honey. I got the recipe from Elsa Decker. She is such a lovely person. I'm so happy she and Fred are thriving with the bakery business."

"I think everyone is happy to see them doing so well, Cleo," Everett said, picking up the book he'd been reading before Gracy arrived.

"Read to us, Papa?" Gracy asked, settling onto a footstool her mother nudged closer to the low table in front of the couch, where she'd set the tray of food. Cleo handed a plate with a wedge of apple pie to Everett, took one for herself, and smiled at Gracy.

A sandwich made of roast beef and sliced cheese, a tangy pickle, and a small bowl of vegetable soup was the perfect meal as Gracy listened to her father read from a new Jack London novel about a young man striving to better himself.

Once she'd eaten her meal and a slice of the apple pie that was still warm from the oven, Gracy grew drowsy in front of the fire. Her eyelids were too heavy to hold open, and her father's voice became an echo in the distance before a hand gently shook her shoulder, dragging her from almost asleep to mostly awake.

"Off to bed with you, darling, before you fall off the stool." Cleo cupped Gracy's chin, then held out a hand to her.

Gracy rose, kissed her mother's cheek, then her father's, and made her way upstairs. Her head barely hit the pillow before sleep claimed her. Rather than being tormented by her disastrous day, she dreamed of Cord striding toward her from his barn while snow danced around them.

Chapter Nine

"Aren't you going to join in the bets of who'll win?" Gracy asked, leaning closer to Cord so he could hear her above the shouts of the crowd that had gathered at Blake and Ginny Stratton's place.

After the snow on Tuesday, the temperatures had plummeted, freezing the shallow end of the pond and making it possible for the annual ice skating event to take place. Blake and Luke had poured buckets of water that froze almost immediately on top of the snow to enlarge the skating area, concerned about anyone skating where the water was deep.

Anyone who was able had ventured out despite the cold to join in the festivities and fun of the day.

Gracy had pulled an old skating outfit from a trunk her father had hauled down from their attic. Surprised it still fit, she was pleased to have something appropriate to wear, even if she hadn't yet decided if she'd skate.

Her mother had insisted she bring her skates along, though, and when she'd spied Cord wearing a pair as he'd stood on the edge of the crowd, watching Blake and Luke prepare to race on the ice, she was glad she'd given in to her mother's commands. She'd quickly slipped on her skates, then hurried to stand next to him.

"I'm not betting or joining in this craziness. Filly and Ginny both warned me to remain neutral today or I'd never hear the end of it." Cord grinned down at her. "If I were betting, I'd put my money on Luke, though, because he's more ruthless and determined than Blake."

Gracy smiled. "I'll be sure to share that with him the next time I see him."

"You will do no such thing, Miss Randall." Cord gave her a warning scowl, then grinned again when Bodie rushed over to him with Cullen and Patrick Granger. The three boys got along well and seemed to take great pleasure in being cousins and playmates.

"Daddy, we can't see the race!" Bodie patted his mittened hands against the front of Cord's coat. "We want to see!"

"Just a minute," Cord said, removing his skates, then bending down. "Hop on, Cullen."

The boy, who was nine, climbed onto Cord's back, wrapping his arms around his neck. Cord lifted Patrick in one arm and Bodie in the other.

"How about now? Can you see?" Cord asked, smiling at Bodie.

"Yep. We can see good!" Bodie said, excitedly bouncing in his father's arms.

"Hold still, or I'll set you all down. Got it?" Cord shifted Bodie slightly.

Gracy admired his strength and ability to hold three boys at the same time. She considered offering to hold Bodie, since he was the youngest, but the boy still sometimes looked at her like she was a dragon about to breathe fire and destruction upon him.

She thought she'd made some headway at winning him over, though, when she'd seen him Thursday for supper. He and Cord had stopped by to ask her father a question about a piece of equipment Cord had found in an old shed, and her mother had insisted they stay for the meal. After they'd eaten, Gracy had sat at the piano, showing Bodie how to play a simple song, then letting him place his hands over hers as she played a few Christmas carols. The little boy seemed to love music of any kind. She'd noticed at church he enjoyed singing the hymns, even if he didn't always belt out the correct words.

"On your mark. Get set. Go!" shouted Pastor Chauncy Dodd as Blake and Luke took off in a mad dash across the ice. They were to skate around a box holding a bright red flag that had been placed fifty yards away, then return to the starting line.

The two men, who acted no more mature than half-grown boys, shoved and pushed, tripped and tormented each other the whole way to the box.

As he circled it, Luke reached out and gave Blake such a mighty push, he sailed right off the ice and rolled in the snow. In seconds, he was back on his feet, careening toward Luke. When he caught up to him, he grabbed the back of Luke's coat and yanked, tossing him into the crowd. Blake might have won if he hadn't looked back and tripped over a branch frozen in the ice.

Gracy couldn't help but laugh at the sight Blake made. He looked like some sort of toy as his arms flailed in circles and his feet tried to go in opposite directions.

A few men who were laughing so hard they could barely stand upright gave Luke a mighty shove that caused him to land on his backside. He slid toward Blake who was still trying to get his feet to work together. Before he could regain his balance, Luke smashed into him, toppling him to the ice.

Blake placed a hand on Luke's face, pushing himself to his feet, but Luke grabbed onto his ankle before he could skate away. Although Blake tried to stand on one foot and shake him off, he nearly landed back on the ice. Luke dragged himself upward, using Blake's leg as a climbing post, then took off toward the finish line.

He was nearly there when Blake skated beside him and jabbed him so hard in the side, Gracy could hear Luke suck in a great wheezing gasp of air.

"You sound like a set of broken bellows," Blake taunted as they closed in on the finish line.

The crowd cheered and clapped, laughing and shouting as the two men battled to win.

Suddenly, Luke stuck out his foot to trip Blake, but his brother-in-law jumped over it, took a few slippery steps, and crashed on the ice, taking Luke down with him. They slid in a heap over the line that had been painted across the ice to declare the winner.

"Aw, they both fell down," Patrick said, his disappointment evident in his expression as he looked at Cord. "Does that mean they both lose?"

"Afraid so," Cord said, setting Patrick and Bodie on their feet, then bending over for Cullen to jump off. "Maybe you should join Seth and Judd in telling your dad and uncle that they both tried hard."

"Okay," Patrick said, rushing off to join Blake and Ginny's sons in helping their father off the ice. Luke held out a hand to Cullen and one to Patrick, letting the boys pull him up.

Filly shook her head and thrust a handkerchief full of snow into Luke's face, making him splutter as she attempted to stop the blood dripping from his nose.

"They do that every year?" Cord asked as he refastened his skates and glanced up at Gracy.

In that moment, Cord looked so young and carefree, he could have been just another of the boys ready for fun instead of a widower with a young son.

Gracy tugged her wits together and nodded. "Every year. They seem to grow more, um, aggressive the older they get."

"Maybe they need some younger blood to challenge them," Cord said, offering her a teasing grin that drew out her smile. "Miss Randall, might you accompany me on a turn across the ice?"

Gracy stared at the arm he held out to her, an arm that had held a little boy eager to watch the skating race just moments earlier. She wondered what it would feel like to have that arm wrapped around her. What it would be like to be a recipient of Cord's affections?

Annoyed with her runaway imagination, she brought herself back to the moment. Accepting Cord's invitation to skate didn't mean anything. They were friends, after all, and friends did that sort of thing.

She placed her hand on his arm, glad her mother had forced her into not only bringing her skates but putting them on earlier. Cord remained close behind her as they moved onto the ice, and the community band played a waltz that was a perfect song for skating.

"You look quite fetching today, Gracy. Is that a new outfit?" Cord asked, glancing down at her with a twinkle in his hazel eyes.

Gracy glanced down at the emerald green skirt with a blue and green plaid jacket. Maybe missing a few meals this week hadn't been so terrible after all. It meant she'd been able to get into her old clothes.

"Thank you, kind sir. The outfit is not new, but I haven't worn it since I left Hardman. Mama made it for me when I was still in high school."

"You must have been a raving beauty even then," Cord said in a low, husky tone as his head dipped close to her ear. "That green color is spectacular on you, Gracy. With your red hair and perfect complexion, you make me think of Christmas."

Pink infused her cheeks, and it wasn't from the cold or the slight breeze but Cord's words.

"You do go on, don't you, Mr. Granger?" she said, giving him what she hoped was a cheeky smile. It had been years since she'd spoken so lightly and freely with a man. Not since Samuel had caught her eye and won her heart. She'd forgotten how satisfying it could be to interact with a man who made her keenly aware of being a woman.

All the years she'd lived in Grass Valley, she'd shut herself off from anyone who showed even the slightest interest in her. Her friends had tried to nudge her past her grief, but she hadn't been able to let go.

Now, as she settled back into the community of Hardman, a place to which she never thought she'd return, she felt a sense of contentment—a peace—she'd never expected to experience. She didn't know if it was being with her parents, old friends, the town, or Cord that had helped her finally move forward, but in the weeks that she'd been home, she had found herself again.

Gracy had always been someone full of smiles and laughter up until Samuel, Rob, and her brother's family had died. She'd felt like all the joy within her had been buried with them. Yet, lately, she could feel it bubbling up inside her again, ready to spill out in unexpected giggles or grins over the silliest things.

Her mother had given her a sharp look just last Sunday at church when Gracy had barely subdued a laugh at the antics of Claire and Grayson Carter's boys, who were seated in front of them. The two little imps had done their best to distract their sister, Maddie, as she played a lovely violin solo of a favored hymn.

Gracy sent up a prayer of thanksgiving to be reclaiming her joy and finding her way back to herself after such a long time of just going through the motions of living.

As Cord moved his hand so it circled her waist and guided her as they skated in unison, she couldn't help but ponder if his presence—his and Bodie's—were part of the reason for her newfound happiness.

"You are a graceful skater, Gracy. Did you do this a lot when you were in school?" Cord asked, drawing her back to the moment.

Gracy thought back to all the fun days of skating with friends and special times she'd participated in at the Stratton family's skating party. "I did. It was always such fun. You may not believe it, based on the day we met, but I used to be quite a jolly girl."

Cord gave her an intense, observant look, then smiled that smile that made him look so boyish and charming. "I could believe it, Gracy. You're a lively, vibrant woman. I assume you've likely always been that way."

Pleased yet embarrassed by his words, she looked off into the distance. "Not always, but I'm trying to find that happiness again."

"Maybe we can work on finding it together," Cord said with his mouth so near to her ear, Gracy could feel the warmth of his breath as it caressed her neck. A shiver slid down her spine and Cord offered her a concerned look. "Are you cold?"

She couldn't very well inform him his nearness made her want to peel off her skating jacket and unwind the scarf she'd wrapped around her neck. "No. I'm fine, but thank you for asking."

"Perhaps we'd better head back," Cord said, applying slight pressure to her waist as he turned them and headed back in the direction of the party. There were a few other couples around them, but the children and older skaters remained close to the food tables, benches, and a roaring bonfire that chased away the winter chill.

They were nearly back to the gathering when Bodie waved and tried to run onto the ice. His feet went out from under him, and he leaned forward, landing on his knees. The boy giggled as he crashed into their legs. Only Cord's athletic abilities kept the three of them from ending up in a heap.

"Let's get some hot chocolate, son, then maybe it's time to teach you how to skate," Cord said, picking up the boy and setting him on his shoulder, then offering the opposite arm to Gracy. She placed her hand on it, looked up at Bodie, and smiled at the happiness radiating from his face.

Despite the fact that she still thought him a bit on the mischievous side, he was undeniably cute and could be quite sweet when the mood struck.

"Do you think we should get a cookie or two to have with the hot chocolate?" Gracy asked as they stepped off the ice, removed their skates, and walked together through the packed snow toward the refreshments.

"Two cookies and a piece of fudge!" Bodie proclaimed, pointing to Filly as she slapped away Luke's hand when he tried to remove the snow-packed handkerchief she continued to hold to his nose. "Aunt Filly made the fudge, and it's yummy."

Cord looked down at his son. "How many pieces of fudge have you had, Bode?"

Bodie glanced down at his feet and swirled the toe of his boot in the snow. "Maybe this many." He held up three fingers.

Cord gave Gracy a look that made it clear he thought Bodie had indulged in more than enough candy. "Let's skip the fudge, and you can have one cookie. Or would you rather have a popcorn ball?"

Bodie cocked his little head and gave his father a curious glance. "How'd they make popcorn in a ball? Can you play with it?"

"No, son, but you can eat it." Cord picked up a small popcorn ball and gave it to Bodie, then lifted a cup of hot chocolate and handed it to Gracy. "Did your mom bring those delicious peppermint drops I like so well?"

Gracy took the hot chocolate from him and nodded. "She did. I think she even kept a few at home in case you don't get any today. She said she'd give them to you tomorrow. Might I assume you are joining us for lunch after the church service?"

Cord nodded and guided Bodie away from the sweets. "Everett invited me to join you when I saw him yesterday. I hope you don't mind."

"Not at all." Gracy refused to admit it, but the thought of spending more time with handsome Cord Granger filled her with anticipation. She looked over to where the doctor was examining Luke's bleeding nose and lecturing Blake, who held a handful of snow to his left eye. Gracy thought Luke's elbow might have connected with it at some point. "Do you think they'll be fine?"

Cord shook his head, then grinned. "The injuries they gave each other won't be an issue, but they both might get tired of having Aunt Dora ream their ears."

Bodie pressed a hand to the side of his knit cap, covering his ear. "I don't want Aunt Dora reaming my ears. Does it hurt?"

Gracy admired the way Cord hunkered down so he was on eye level with Bodie and placed a hand on his son's shoulder. "It's just an expression, Bodie, that means she'll tell them they didn't behave very well today. Aunt Dora would never do anything to hurt you."

"Okay." Bodie took a sip of his hot chocolate, leaving a ring of it around his mouth. "Can I play with Patrick now?"

Cord straightened and looked over to where Patrick and a few of the other small children built a snowman. "Sure, you go on, but leave your chocolate here if you're finished."

Bodie took another gulp of the chocolate, shoved his half-eaten cookie in his mouth, and raced off to join his cousin and friends.

"You're so good with him, Cord. Most parents aren't as thoughtful and compassionate with their children," Gracy said, as they watched Bodie laugh at something Patrick said.

"I just try to treat him the way I like to be treated. I know I probably let him get away with things I shouldn't, but he's just so curious about everything and so smart. It doesn't take him long to catch on to anything I've shown him."

"Mama and Papa think he's quite something. Thank you for sharing him with them. It truly means the world to them to have a young one to dote on again."

With a humble shrug, Cord set their empty chocolate cups on a table and guided Gracy over to listen as Maddie Carter performed a few songs on her violin. The first one was a haunting, slow tune that made emotion well in Gracy until she thought she might drown in it. The second song was a classical piece Gracy recognized from her own years of playing the piano. The third tune was so lively, it seemed every toe was tapping and, in fact, a few couples and several of the younger children danced across the hard-packed snow.

When Cord took Gracy in his arms and swung her around, a laugh made of pure joy bubbled out of her. Snow kicked up beneath the feet of the dancers and swirled in the air in a powdery haze that added to the wonder of the moment.

The song ended amid whistles and cheers from the crowd, then Blake thanked everyone for attending and expressed his wishes for them to have a safe journey home. The temperature had plummeted again, and for the safety of all attending, it was time to leave.

Gracy felt as though every one of her nerves thrummed with energy after dancing with Cord. It had been such a carefree, lovely moment. She'd long remember it with fondness regardless of what the future might bring.

She saw a flash of something in his eyes as he turned to her. It could have been yearning, or perhaps it was regret.

He smiled at her and took her hand in his, removed the mitten she wore, and kissed the backs of her fingers. "Thank you for today, Gracy. It's the most fun I've had in a long while."

"I … um …" Gracy felt incapable of getting her brain and tongue to work in conjunction with one another. Not when Cord continued to hold her fingers captive and looked at her with a warm light flickering in his eyes.

"Daddy! Can I ride with Patrick?" Bodie asked, running up to them and patting Cord's leg to draw his attention.

Cord gave her one last look, one she knew held longing, before he slipped the mitten back on her hand and released it. He picked up Bodie and shook his head. "No, Bode. We need to head on home. Why don't you go on in the house with Seth and

Judd for a little while, though, until I'm ready to leave."

"Okay!" Bodie squirmed to get down and raced off after Seth and Judd who were heading inside the house with their mother. The two boys were closer to Cullen's age than Bodie's, but they welcomed him with pleased smiles as they trooped in out of the cold.

"I should go see what I can do to help Blake with the cleanup." Cord backed away a step. "I guess I'll see you tomorrow at church."

"Yes. I'll be there." Gracy watched Cord back away a few more steps. Before he turned and strode off, though, she placed a hand on his arm, stopping him. He looked at her in question, and she smiled. "I had a wonderful time today as well, Cord. Thank you."

He grinned and nodded his head. "I'm glad, Gracy. Stay warm on the trip back to town."

Gracy knew all she'd have to do was think of the way he kissed her fingers, and she'd be toasty in no time.

Chapter Ten

"I can't believe anyone with a lick of sense would do such a thing," Cleo said, leaning back in her chair and pressing a hand to her throat. "I can hardly fathom how a woman alone would undertake such a grueling prospect."

Cord shrugged and wiped his mouth on his napkin. "I suppose desperation will drive people to do most anything. I'm not certain Miss Byron is alone, though. From the article, it sounded like someone would travel along with her in a wagon with supplies."

"I agree about desperation driving people to do strange things," Everett said, helping himself to another dinner roll. Gracy was pleased her father seemed to enjoy them. She'd worked hard to make sure they were as good as the rolls her mother always made. "For a young woman to travel more than five hundred miles in cold, snowy weather, she truly must be in a dire need of the funds."

"Still, for a woman of any age to undertake such an adventure just to win a wager seems rather fickle." Cleo glanced at Gracy. "I'm grateful our girl has more sense than doing something like that."

Gracy rather admired Miss Byron for setting out on the trek from Shoshone, Idaho, to Denver, Colorado, to prove to her wealthy uncle it was possible. If she succeeded in the journey, her uncle had promised to give her ten thousand dollars. From the information Gracy had gleaned from the article, Miss Byron intended to use the money to pay off the debts against her family's farm and open a home for orphans. Either reason alone was quite inspiring, but the fact she intended to do both made Gracy silently cheer for the young woman to succeed in her endeavors.

Everett bumped Gracy's arm with his elbow. "You're being awfully quiet, girlie. What do you think of Miss Byron's wager?"

"I hope she succeeds, not just so she'll have the money for the farm and the orphanage, but also to prove that anyone, regardless of age or gender, can accomplish anything they set their minds to."

Cord offered her an encouraging smile as he helped himself to another piece of roast and a second serving of mashed potatoes. Gracy had made the gravy and watched as he ladled a generous spoon of it over the potatoes.

"Wasn't there a gentleman who walked across the country earlier this year?" Cleo questioned as she passed Everett a bowl of creamed peas.

Everett nodded. "Yes. Edward Payson Weston walked from New York to California in just a little more than one hundred days. He'd hoped to make it in a hundred, but some unexpected delays prohibited him from making his goal."

Cord glanced up from his plate. "Isn't he the fellow who gained notoriety for walking from Portland, Maine, to Chicago in less than a month?"

Everett nodded. "That's the one. He was known as the most famous American pedestrian of the previous century. From the stories I've read, he was not a particularly strong child and took up walking to improve his health. He eventually began walking for competition. He even competed in England. He embarked on his latest adventure in March on his seventieth birthday. I think it's quite something he not only attempted a transcontinental journey but succeeded."

"It was a note-worthy adventure." Cord lifted his glass of grape juice. "To worthwhile endeavors and the friends who cheer us on."

"Here, here!" Everett said, toasting his glass to Cleo's, then Cord's, and Gracy's. Bodie lifted his glass of milk, and Cord helped him toast everyone without spilling it.

Gracy had been impressed with Bodie's table manners. The little boy had a good appetite and generally ate quietly without interrupting the adults. He knew to say please and thank you, and used his napkin, although often it was with more spirit than skill. When he was indoors, he behaved well and minded his elders. But outside, he tended to run a little wild.

At his age, Gracy couldn't really blame him. He needed to do something to run off all the excess energy he seemed to bottle up indoors.

She smiled at Bodie and returned her attention to her father and Cord discussing an article in the newspaper about quail becoming a nuisance in a Seattle suburb, and the thousands of ducks, geese, and swans that had overtaken Tillamook Bay on the Oregon coast.

"Too bad we don't have time to make a trip that way to go hunting. We could bring home a fat goose for Christmas," Everett said, looking at Cleo. "Are you planning to fix a goose or turkey, or something else for Christmas, wife?"

Cleo narrowed her gaze as she looked at Everett. "Perhaps we'll have oatmeal and toast, and I'll take the day off from cooking."

Everett laughed as though she told a great joke until her gaze narrowed even more. He glanced at Gracy, and she feigned innocence. She and her mother had already discussed in length their menu for Christmas Eve and Christmas Day. They'd been invited to join the Granger family at Granger House for Christmas Day and had coordinated with Filly on the dishes they'd bring. Apparently, though, her father had not been made aware of the plans.

"Maybe just day-old slices of bread with some meat and cheese would do," Gracy teased, knowing how much her father loved turkey with all the trimmings including pumpkin and apple pies.

At his crestfallen look, Cleo laughed and patted his arm. "We'll be having a turkey on Christmas Eve. I ordered one a month ago from the Osbourne family. They have the best turkeys. We'll have all the trimmings, including cranberry sauce and pumpkin pie, after the church service. As for Christmas dinner, we've been invited to join the Granger family at Granger House. Filly asked us to bring dinner rolls, a squash casserole, and peppermint drop cookies. Gracy is also going to make a chocolate layered cake and corn pudding."

Everett appeared relieved to know his holiday meal would be as wonderful as always, then he looked over at Cord. "The girls had me worried for a moment. If you have no other plans on Christmas Eve, you and Bodie are welcome to join us."

"Thank you, sir. We've been invited to spend the evening at Aunt Dora's house, but we'll see. We might just stay at the ranch and eat in the bunkhouse with Tug and the others."

Cleo shook her head. "Oh, that won't do. You'll be in town for the Christmas Eve service anyway, and you must attend the Christmas Eve Carnival at your aunt's home that afternoon. It's one of the events the community looks forward to all year." She abruptly switched topics in the conversation. "Have you had any luck finding a cook or housekeeper?"

Cord shook his head. "None so far, then again, I haven't put much effort into looking. I figure people might be more interested in starting new positions after the holidays."

"Perhaps," Cleo said, then turned toward Gracy.

The look on her mother's face made Gracy want to squirm. It wasn't her fault, exactly, that she'd been unable to find gainful employment. After the disastrous experiences at the skating rink and the restaurant, Gracy had worked for a day at the assay office, until two of the men who came in wouldn't take no for an answer and a fight had broken out. The office manager had told her she was too much of a distraction and sent her home. She'd worked for one day helping Filly decorate Granger House for the holidays, but that was more fun than work. And Friday, she'd spent a good part of the day helping her mother clean the house and do the baking she usually saw to on Saturday so they could spend the day enjoying the skating party.

Gracy felt an urgent, pressing need to find a job, one that would last more than a few hours or days. She thought about traveling to a larger town or even a city if something didn't work out soon in Hardman. However, thoughts of leaving town when she was starting to feel so much more like herself made her hesitant to even consider moving away again. Hardman was and would likely always be her home no matter where she lived.

"Gracy made a new pie recipe she found in a magazine Brynn Rutherford gave her the other day," Cleo said, rising from the table. "Are you gents ready for dessert?"

"Always," Everett said, catching Cleo's hand and kissing her palm. "With some coffee?"

"Of course." Cleo turned to Cord. "Coffee for you?"

"Yes, please." Cord reached for Bodie's empty plate and stacked it with his, then started to rise, but Gracy hurried to take the plates and scurried into the kitchen.

Cleo filled cups with coffee and set them on a tray, carrying it to the dining room, while Gracy set the pie and dessert plates along with forks and a pie server on a second tray. After she'd cut and served the pie, she waited for her father or Cord to say something. When they ate in silence, she wondered if the pie hadn't turned out well. She'd been careful to follow each step exactly as the recipe was given. If she cared to admit it, she'd wanted to impress Cord with her baking. She wasn't as good as her mother, and nowhere nearly as talented in the kitchen as Filly Granger, but she could cook well enough that the food was filling and flavorful.

Gracy watched as her mother cut off a small bite of the pie on her plate and sampled it, then took a drink of her coffee.

Unable to stand it, Gracy cut off a piece of her pie and was about to take a bite when Bodie held his plate out to her. "More, please?"

She smiled at the little boy. "You liked it?"

"Uh, huh. It's yummy!" Bodie rubbed a hand around on his tummy.

"Then you should have a little more," Gracy said, smiling at him as she placed a small piece of pie on his plate and set the plate in front of him.

She glanced around the table, then took a bite of the pie. It was better than she'd anticipated, rich with custard filling and nutmeg.

Her father looked at her and winked. "Bet you thought we didn't like it."

"Your silence definitely made me question if I'd somehow wrecked the recipe." Gracy bumped her shoulder against her father's. "If you like nutmeg, it's quite tasty."

"I think we all like nutmeg and would agree it is a recipe you should make again," her mother said, offering Gracy a pleased smile. "Speaking of making things again, did I mention …"

Gracy let her thoughts ramble while her mother talked and Cord and Everett interjected comments as they enjoyed dessert.

They'd barely finished eating the pie when Cleo glanced at the clock on the wall. "Gracious, we should get going, Everett. I promised Martha we'd be out to see them early this afternoon." She turned to Gracy. "Your father and I are going out to visit Mr. and Mrs. Berglund this afternoon. We'll be back before dark. Would you mind cleaning up the dishes? I planned to have leftover ham for supper. I've got a pot of beans to go with it simmering slow on the back of the stove."

"That's fine, Mama," Gracy rose and kissed her mother's cheek. "Have a wonderful time visiting Mr. and Mrs. Berglund and tell them I said hello."

"We'll do that, honey," Everett said, rising and shaking Cord's hand. "Don't feel like you need to rush off, Cord, just because we're leaving. If you like, let Bodie take a rest before you head home."

Gracy looked over and saw Bodie fighting to keep his eyes open, even as he held his last bite of pie almost to his lips. Cord took the fork from Bodie's fingers, ate the pie, then reached to pick up his son, but Bodie looked to Cleo and held out his arms.

"I want Grammy to sing me a song," Bodie whispered, his eyes already drifting shut.

"Of course, sweetheart." Cleo lifted the boy in her arms, kissed his temple, and carried him down the hall to the bedroom she and Everett shared. She returned a few minutes later, a soft look on her face that Gracy only saw when she was with Bodie. "He fell asleep as soon as I laid him down."

"He'll likely nap for an hour," Cord said, picking up dishes off the dining table. "I can help Gracy with the dishes while you two go for your visit. Give my regards to Mr. and Mrs. Berglund."

"We will," Cleo said, kissing Gracy's cheek as she passed through the kitchen, picking up a basket full of baked goods to take with her.

Gracy listened to the soft murmur of her parents' voices as they bundled into their coats, then the quiet click of the door as they left.

"Looks like you're stuck with me until—" The jangling of the telephone interrupted Cord.

Gracy had soap suds halfway to her elbows, so she tipped her head toward the telephone. "Would you mind answering?"

"Happy to," Cord said, rushing to answer before it jangled again and woke Bodie. "Randall residence."

Cord turned to her and grinned. "Oh, hey, Luke."

Gracy couldn't hear what was said, but as Cord's expression turned from amused to concerned, she assumed something was wrong.

"I'll be right there." Cord hung up the earpiece and rolled down his shirtsleeves. "There's a fire at the Bisbee farm. They need all the help they can get. Would you mind if I leave Bodie here?"

"No. Go on. We'll be fine. If you want, take my horse, Cider. It might be faster than driving your auto out there on these slick roads." Gracy didn't lightly offer the use of her beloved horse to just anyone, but Cider was fast and sure-footed.

"Thank you, Gracy, but if the fire is bad, Cider will be safer here. I'll take my auto, but I do appreciate the offer, and I'm grateful to you for keeping an eye on Bodie. I don't know when I'll be back."

"We'll be fine, I'm sure. Just be careful." Gracy wanted to give Cord a hug, to tell him she'd be praying for him and the others to stay safe, but she returned to washing dishes as Cord yanked on his coat. "You could wear Papa's old chore coat if you don't want to take a chance on ruining yours."

"I don't think it would fit, but thanks for offering. I'll be back as soon as I can." Cord tugged on his hat and was out the door before Gracy could utter a word. She leaned forward, watching out the kitchen window as he raced around the porch and out to where he'd left his auto parked. She heard it chug to life and knew he'd hustle out to the Bisbee place to lend a hand. She hoped the fire was soon contained and it wasn't burning the house.

Gracy decided it might be helpful to prepare food for those who were out fighting the fire. She had no idea how many were there, but she stoked the fire in the cookstove and set about making a double batch of biscuits. With the ham her mother had baked on Friday and left in the refrigerator for their supper tonight, she could make sandwiches. Once the biscuits came out of the oven, she'd whip up some molasses cookies. She was certain someone would be heading out to the farm with food before evening arrived.

The biscuits were just browned to perfection when she heard a noise and looked over to see Bodie standing in the doorway, rubbing sleep from his eyes as his lip rolled out in a pout.

"Where's my daddy?" he asked, glancing around the kitchen.

"He went to help Luke with something," she said, unwilling to frighten the child by telling him there was a fire.

"Where's Grammy and Gramps?" Bodie looked hesitant to walk into the kitchen or any closer to her.

"They went to visit friends." Gracy smiled at him as she set the pans of biscuits on the counter to cool. "Would you like to help me make cookies?"

Bodie stared at her a long moment before he slid one sock-covered foot a little closer to her. "What kind of cookies?"

"I was thinking about making molasses cookies, but maybe we should make something else. What's your favorite kind?"

Bodie grinned. "I like doodles!"

"Doodles?" Gracy asked, then realized he meant snickerdoodles. The cinnamon and sugar-topped cookie was also one of her favorites. She'd gotten the recipe from a friend in Grass Valley and shared it with her mother a few years ago. Her mother must have made the treat for Bodie before. "Snickerdoodles?"

"Yeah. Doodles!" Bodie took a few cautious steps closer. "Can we make doodles?"

"We certainly can," Gracy said, then began gathering the ingredients for the cookies. "How about we wash your hands and roll up your sleeves so you can help?"

"Okay!" Bodie raced down the hall, and Gracy followed him to the bathroom where he'd pulled himself up and balanced on his belly on the edge of the sink, flinging water and soap as he washed his hands. Rather than chastise him, Gracy picked up a thick towel and held it out to him once he'd rinsed off the soap. "Good job, Bodie. Let's dry your hands, then you can help me make the cookies."

The little boy stood still as she dried his hands, then he raced back to the kitchen. Gracy took a second to mop up the splashes on the floor and wipe away the soap suds dripping down the mirror above the sink before she returned to the kitchen.

Bodie had pushed up his shirtsleeves and was trying to tie a dish towel around his waist for an apron.

"How about I help you with that?" Gracy took the towel from him, knotting it at his waist. "Are you ready to make cookies?"

"Cookies!" Bodie shouted, then giggled as he dragged a chair over to the counter and climbed on it so he could watch her every move. Gracy broke two eggs into a bowl and lightly beat them, then let Bodie help her measure butter, sugar, flour, cream of tartar, and soda. She let him stir the batter, placing her hand above his on the spoon to guide his movements. When he looked up at her with a happy grin, her heart felt like wax left too near to a fire— soft and melting.

"Now we spoon the dough onto the baking sheet," she said, handing him a smaller spoon and showing him how to drop the dough. "Then we sprinkle sugar and cinnamon on top."

"I like this part best," Bodie said, licking his finger, then dipping it into the cup of sugar and cinnamon Gracy had mixed together. He popped it into his mouth and giggled again.

"You are a scamp," Gracy said, gently tapping his nose, drawing out his infectious laughter.

"Can we eat them now?" Bodie asked, reaching for a mound of dough.

"First, they have to bake, but it won't take long," she said, sliding two pans of cookies into the oven. While they baked, she whipped up a second batch of cookies.

"They smell good," Bodie said, snitching a bite of dough and rolling it in the sugar and cinnamon before he shoved it into his mouth. Gracy joined him in eating a bit of the dough before she took the cookies from the oven and slid in two more pans of cookies.

"Would you like to go outside and play awhile, Bodie? We need to give the cookies time to cool before we can eat them."

"Can we sled?" Bodie asked as he hopped off the chair and started for the hooks by the back door, where his coat hung.

"Yes, we can, but first you need to wash the dough off your hands, and we can't go out until the cookies come out of the oven." Gracy lifted him up to the kitchen sink and helped him wash his hands. She breathed in the scent of little boy that smelled like soap and sunshine and adventure, grinning as he haphazardly dried his hands before she set him down.

Bodie gave her an odd look as she washed the dishes they'd dirtied making the cookies, but he didn't run off. While she dried the dishes and put them away, he stood in front of the oven, staring at it, as though his focused attention would make the cookies cook faster.

"Let's get your boots on, then you'll be ready when the cookies come out of the oven," Gracy said, retrieving his boots from the hall and sitting down on a kitchen chair.

Bodie skipped over to her and plopped onto the floor, reaching for a boot. Gracy helped him get them both on, then stood, and he jumped up, racing over to the oven.

"Are they ready?" he asked, his face and voice full of hopeful anticipation.

Gracy peeked into the oven and nodded. "They are. You stand back so you don't get burned while I pull them out."

Bodie obediently backed up a few paces, then Gracy took the cookies from the oven and left them to cool on the counter.

"Now can we go outside?"

Gracy nodded. "Yes. Get your coat and hat and your mittens."

Bodie ran into the hall and rammed his hands into the sleeves of his coat. His mittens were on a long yarn string that ran through his sleeves, so Gracy adjusted them and helped him get them on. She pulled the stocking cap over his thick brown hair and hurried to slip on her own boots and coat and snagged a scarf on the way out the door.

The old wooden sled she'd used as a child was stored in the loft of the barn.

Gracy yanked on her mittens, wrapped the scarf around her head to cover her ears, then looped it around her neck, and held a hand out to Bodie. "Let's go get a sled, and I'll give you a ride."

"Yippee!" Bodie whooped and ran ahead to the barn.

Bentley lifted his aged head from his bed on the back porch and woofed once, as though he wished he felt up to playing in the snow. Gracy stopped to give the old dog a loving pat or two, then rushed after Bodie as he bounded toward the barn.

Although the November weather had been mild, December had been cold and snowy. With the temperatures still so frigid and snow falling every other day or so, they were in for a white Christmas.

Honestly, she was glad. It just didn't seem like the holiday season without snow on the ground. But once the new year rolled around, it could melt and warm up to spring-like temperatures, and she wouldn't complain at all.

When Gracy caught up to Bodie, he was trying to pull open the barn door but lacked the strength to do it.

"I'll help," Gracy said, reaching above Bodie to open the door. He scurried inside ahead of her. "I think the sled is up in the loft."

"I know where it is. Gramps showed it to me last time I climbed up there." Bodie started up the ladder before Gracy could stop him. She debated between following him to make sure he didn't get hurt or letting him feel like he had done something important by retrieving it.

When Bodie scooted over the edge into the loft, Gracy stepped back until she could see him. He went straight for the corner where she could see the sled propped against the wall.

"Can you reach it?" she asked.

"Yep! I gots it!" Bodie called down to her. She heard wood scraping against wood, then the crash of metal.

"Are you hurt, Bodie?"

"I knocked over that old milk can with the hole in it."

Gracy had no idea there was a milk can up there, but she was glad Bodie was unharmed. "That's fine. Can you scoot the sled to the edge? I'll grab it."

"Here it comes," Bodie said, giving the sled a push. Gracy leaped up as it sailed over the edge and caught it by the rope tied to the front handles.

Bodie giggled above her. "Can you do that again?"

"No," she said, leaning the sled against the wall, then looking up at him. "Do you need help getting down?"

"I can do it," Bodie said, turning around and carefully feeling for the ladder with his toes. When they were on the first step, he started down. Like a little monkey, he shimmied down each rung and tugged on Gracy's hand as soon as he reached the ground. "Come on! Let's go!"

"Coming," Gracy said, picking up the sled and following him outside. After she shut the barn door, she placed the sled on the snow and Bodie hopped onto it, then gave her an expectant look.

"Now you pull it," he said, settling onto his backside with his little hands gripping the sides of the sled.

"I do?" Gracy asked, pretending she had no idea what he wanted.

"Yes. You pull the string, and I get to ride."

Gracy frowned as she picked up the rope attached to the handle. "That doesn't seem very fair. Who pulls me? When do I get a ride?"

Bodie appeared thoughtful. "I know! My daddy can give you a ride when he gets back."

Gracy had a vision of Cord pulling her and Bodie, all three of them laughing, and it warmed her from the heart outward.

"Hang on," she cautioned Bodie, then began pulling the sled. She pulled it all around the little pasture, but after a few minutes, Bodie seemed eager for something more exciting. "I have an idea, Bodie. Would you be willing to ride the sled with me?"

"Sure," he said, scooting forward.

She smiled and held a hand out to him. "First, we have to take the sled out to a hill, then we can ride it."

"Okay!" He rolled off the sled and into the snow, giggling as he got to his feet, then grabbed onto her hand. "Where is the hill?"

Gracy recalled sledding by the school in her younger years and decided it would be a good spot. There might even be other children playing there. "By the school," she said, and headed in that direction, then stopped. "We'd better leave a note in case your father or my parents return and wonder where we've gone."

"Notes are good," Bodie said, skipping beside her as they returned to the house.

Gracy wrote a quick note and left it on the counter, gave the beans simmering on the back of the stove a quick stir, and yanked her mittens on again.

"Now we can go," she said, once again taking Bodie's hand in hers as they hurried down the sidewalk.

Bodie kept her entertained, telling a story about a fox and a raccoon that were best friends and lived in the woods near Hardman. Gracy thought he had a clever imagination and asked questions that kept him talking as they made their way to the school.

Several children were there, some with their parents, others old enough to come alone. Peals of laughter and teasing made for a lighthearted atmosphere. One of the parents had built a fire, and a big kettle of apple cider scented the air with a delicious aroma.

Gracy watched as a few older children rode down the hill with younger siblings. She even saw Fred Decker on a sled with his twins and decided no one would care if she rode with Bodie. The boy would likely do fine on his own, but Gracy wanted to experience the thrill of racing down the hill again, the wind whipping her cheeks and snow swirling around her.

"This way, Bodie," she said, leading him up the path to the top of the hill. From there, they could see the town of Hardman below them. Gracy drew in a deep breath and looked around, enjoying the sight of a place she'd once hated but now loved.

"We go down that?" Bodie asked, pointing to the hill where others zoomed along the snow-packed surface, laughing as they hurtled toward the bottom.

"We sure do." Gracy noticed the frown line on his forehead and wondered what he was thinking. "If you don't want to go, we don't have to. It's okay to be scared. I was frightened the first time I went down the hill, but my big brother rode with me and made sure I safely reached the bottom. How about if I ride with you, Bodie? Would that be okay?"

The little boy nodded his head.

"Shall we give it a whirl?" Gracy asked, smiling at Bodie.

He nodded again.

Gracy took his hand in hers, and together, they got in line. When it was their turn, Gracy looked at some of the bigger boys who stood ready to give anyone who needed it a push. "Jeff, will you give us a gentle push once we get settled?"

"Sure, Miss Randall," a lanky boy said, moving close behind the sled. He held onto the back of it as Gracy did her best to settle her skirts in a lady-like fashion, then Bodie plopped down on her outstretched legs.

Gracy pulled the rope on the handle tight in her mittened hands. "You hang onto the rope too, Bodie."

Bodie wrapped his hands around the rope, scooched a little closer to Gracy, and glanced back at her with a pitiful look that nearly broke her heart. She could see fear and questions in his gaze. "It'll be fine. I promise," she said.

Bodie bravely nodded his head a third time.

Gracy made sure her arms were securely settled around the child in her care before she glanced over her shoulder. "Go ahead, Jeff. Give us a nudge."

Jeff did more than nudge them, giving them a huge push that sent them flying down the hill at a speed that stole the breath right out of Gracy.

Trees blurred in the periphery of her vision, and powdery snow stung her eyes, but she kept her focus on the bottom of the hill. If she wasn't careful, they'd plow right into the base of the schoolhouse.

"Go, Miss Randall!" she heard some of the older boys yelling. When the sled continued to gain speed, she considered the best way for her and Bodie to bail off without causing him injury.

Thankfully, she was spared the need to do so. When they reached the bottom of the hill, she leaned far to the left, and the sled cut around, plowing into a bank of snow.

Bodie sat perfectly still for several seconds before giggles burst out of him and he hopped off the sled. "That was fun! Let's do it again!"

Gracy was certain her cheeks were as red as her windblown hair, but she'd had too much fun to refuse.

She and Bodie rode the sled down the hill twice more before they took a break by the fire and enjoyed cups of hot cider.

"Can we go again?" Bodie asked, tugging on her hand.

"Once more, then we need to go home," she said, letting him lead her back up the hill.

Several of the other children had already gone home, so they didn't have long to wait for a turn. They were just getting settled on the sled when Gracy felt hands on her back, nudging her forward on the sled.

She glanced back to see Cord's smiling face as he settled behind her, wrapping his arms around her waist.

"You have room for one more?" he asked in a husky voice that made tendrils of warmth curl through her from head to toe.

"Of course," she said, smiling at him over her shoulder.

Bodie leaned around her and flapped a hand at his father. "Hi, Daddy! We're having fun!"

"I can see that, Bode. I'm glad you've had a good time." Cord winked at Gracy, pulling her snugly against his chest.

Sensations she'd never experienced poured over her, and for a moment she felt lightheaded. She wasn't certain her proximity to Cord on the sled was at all appropriate, but there was little to be done about it at the moment unless she wanted to order him off the sled, which she did not.

Even though he smelled of smoke, she welcomed the warmth of his presence at her back. Something about having his arms encircling her waist and his chin resting on her shoulder felt so right and familiar, as if they'd ridden that way dozens of times before.

"Here we go," Cord said as two of the youngsters waiting for their turn gave them a mighty shove.

With the added weight, they flew down the hill, and Gracy squealed with excitement. Bodie laughed the whole way down, even when she and Cord leaned to the left and they crashed into a snowbank, sending snow showering all around them.

Bodie sat up and shook his head, dislodging snow from his ear. Gracy wiped it from her face, unable to see for a moment as it clung to her eyelashes.

"You look like a missus snowman," Bodie said, pointing to Gracy when he rolled off her lap and stood beside the sled.

"You look like a little snowman," Gracy said, making a silly face and reaching for Bodie, causing him to wiggle and giggle.

Cord gave her a questioning glance as he scooted away from her and gained his feet, holding out both hands to help her up.

"Thank you," she said as she brushed snow from her skirt and arms. "I hope I didn't keep Bodie out too long. He was having such fun—we both were—I hated to end it too soon."

"He's used to being outside with me," Cord said, taking the rope to the sled in his hand as the three of them started walking toward the Randall house.

Bodie flopped onto his belly on the sled. "Pull me, Daddy!"

"I'm pulling, Bode. You think Miss Gracy should ride with you?"

"Sure!" Bodie grinned up at her.

"Thank you kindly, Bodie, but I do believe it would be best if I walk home. If your daddy pulls me all that way, his arm might get stretched right out of the socket."

Bodie's eyes widened. "Really?" he asked.

Cord winked at Gracy, then looked back at his son. "I guess I'd look pretty funny with one arm that was ten feet long."

"Yep!" Bodie agreed, then turned so he rested on his back. He stuck his hands behind his head and stared up at the sky. It was still light out, but dusk was fast approaching. "There's a cloud that looks like Cluck-Cluck."

"Cluck-Cluck?" Gracy whispered to Cord.

"His pet chicken." Cord muttered under his breath, then tipped his head to study the sky. "Which one is it, Bode?"

"That one, right there. See it, Gracy?"

Gracy looked up at the sky, but for the life of her couldn't pick out a chicken-shaped cloud. However, she wouldn't do anything to dim Bodie's happy afternoon. "I believe I do see it, Bodie. That's an interesting shape for a cloud, isn't it?"

"Uh, huh."

Gracy glanced at Cord as they stood on a corner and waited for a big wagon to pass by. "Did you get the fire put out?"

"Yes. It was a chimney fire. Fortunately, someone was in the outhouse and saw it before it got away from them. A neighbor called the volunteer fire department, and the fire was contained before it did too much damage. The roof will have to be replaced on part of the house, and one bedroom wall was scorched, but it could have been so much worse." Cord glanced back at Bodie before he looked at Gracy. "If the fire had started at night while they were sleeping, I hate to think what might have happened."

"It would have been tragic. Papa said several people reported squirrels or birds building nests in their chimneys this year. He thinks it's a sign of a long, cold winter."

Cord nodded. "I heard the same thing. Just to be safe, I cleaned our chimney twice, but it's a concern, having a chimney fire."

"It is, but I'm glad the Bisbee family is safe. I made biscuits, and we have a ham I can slice if we should take food out there."

"And cookies!" Bodie added to the conversation.

Gracy turned and smiled at him, then looked back at Cord. "And cookies. Bodie helped me make snickerdoodles. He said they are his favorite."

Cord looked back at his son. "He does enjoy your mom's doodles, as he calls them. She said she got the recipe from you. Do you enjoy baking?"

"Sometimes. I didn't have much time or opportunity when I lived in Grass Valley, but on occasion, I enjoyed preparing a nice meal or making treats for my friends. I got the recipe for snickerdoodles from one of my friends who worked at the telephone office there. Do you have a favorite cookie?"

"I've never turned down molasses cookies or sugar cookies or oatmeal cookies with nuts and raisins."

"It sounds to me like you'll eat just about any ol' cookie," Gracy observed as they arrived at her parents' home. Cord pulled the sled around to the backyard, and Bodie bailed off.

Cord tapped the sled on the ground to knock off the loose snow, then leaned it against the porch.

"Why don't you come in and warm up a while?" Gracy asked, leading the way up the steps and opening the back door. The smell of the simmering beans blended with the cinnamon-laden air from the cookies she and Bodie had baked.

"Mmm, it sure smells good in here," Cord said, following his son inside. He helped Bodie out of his coat and boots, removed his son's mittens and stocking cap, then gave Bodie a nudge toward the bathroom before he turned and held Gracy's coat for her as she slid her arms from the sleeves.

The bottom foot of her skirt was crusted with snow, and her hair was most likely snarled as she unwound the scarf from her head, but she felt full of energy.

"Please excuse me a minute while I put on something dry. If Bodie's clothes are damp, I'm sure I can find something for him to wear." Gracy backed down the hallway so she could rush upstairs.

"Your mom keeps a few clothes for him in the spare room upstairs. I'll see to him," Cord said, then headed toward the bathroom, where Bodie could be heard humming.

Gracy turned and raced up the steps, hastening to her bedroom, and rushed to change into dry clothes in record time. She took a minute to unpin her hair, comb out the tangles, and pin it up again before she hurried downstairs. She found Bodie and Cord in the front room, stoking the fire that had nearly gone out in her absence. Thankfully, her parents had a coal-fed furnace that kept the house warm even without the fireplace.

"There's nothing quite like a fire in the winter to chase away the chill," Cord said, draping Bodie's coat over a chair near the fireplace. He'd left his boots and Bodie's by the fire to dry.

"I agree. Would you like a cup of coffee or tea?" Gracy asked as she edged toward the doorway.

"Either is fine, but if you'd prefer tea, I wouldn't turn down a cup." Cord smiled at her as he picked up Bodie and draped him over one broad shoulder, making his son laugh.

Cord followed Gracy to the kitchen, where she made tea, added a few drops to a cup of milk for Bodie, and served cookies.

"Should I go ahead and make ham and biscuit sandwiches to take out to the Bisbee place?" Gracy asked as Cord broke a cookie in half and handed part of it to Bodie.

"I think that would be nice. I could drop off the food on my way home since it's right on the way. There were a few volunteers planning to stay a while to make sure the fire was out."

"It won't take me long to make them," Gracy said as she set to work slicing ham. Cord got up and retrieved a knife and cut the biscuits in half, and together, they made the sandwiches. Gracy packed them into a basket, then filled another basket with cookies.

"I reckon we'd better head for home before it gets too dark," Cord said, finishing his tea. "Thanks for keeping an eye on Bodie today."

"It was my pleasure. We had a grand time." She smiled at the boy as he dunked his cookie and slurped the liquid from it before it crumbled into his cup. Gracy handed him a spoon and he fished out the chunks, humming as he ate them, then slurping the last of the milky tea.

"Come on, son, we'd better get on the road home." Cord retrieved Bodie's coat from the front room, along with their boots.

"Will he catch a chill in those wet boots?" Gracy asked, suddenly concerned for Bodie's welfare.

"I think he'll be okay, but if you have an extra blanket I can wrap him in, I wouldn't refuse it."

Gracy took two woolen blankets from her mother's tidy linen closet and set them by the door. Cord helped Bodie with his coat and mittens, then gave his son a little push toward her.

"Tell Miss Gracy thank you for today, son."

Bodie crossed the floor and wrapped his arms around her waist. He looked up at her with a big smile that left her heart feeling like warm syrup. "Thank you, Gracy, for making doodles, and letting me eat the dough, and going sledding. It was the best day, and I love you."

On the verge of tears, Gracy dropped to her knees and pulled Bodie into a hug, kissing his cheek, and then brushing the hair back at the cowlick by his left temple. "You are so welcome, Bodie. I had a wonderful time with you. I hope you'll come back and make cookies with me again."

"Yes!" the little boy said, then snatched his stocking cap out of Cord's hand and bounded outside.

Cord hurried to yank on his coat and hat, took the baskets Gracy had filled with food for the Bisbee family, and backed toward the door.

"I can't thank you enough for watching him, Gracy. I hope you meant what you said and did have fun today."

"We had a great time, Cord. I think Bodie is an amazing boy." Gracy picked up the blankets and started to follow him out to his automobile, then she remembered she had slippers on her feet that would get soaked in a second if she stepped any further onto the porch.

Cord set the baskets in the back seat, let Bodie help him start the auto, then jogged back to grab the blankets.

"Thank you, Gracy, for everything." Cord pecked her cheek, took the porch steps in two long strides, and ran around the automobile. After he'd wrapped Bodie in a cocoon of blankets, the two of them waved before heading up the street.

Gracy stood in the open doorway, waving as the two Granger males drove off, each of them holding a huge piece of her heart.

Chapter Eleven

"Well, blast it all anyway," Cord groused as he walked into the kitchen with an armload of wood.

The oatmeal he'd set to cook boiled over in a sticky, gooey mess on the stove. That was bad enough, but the scorched smell was horrid. Cord dumped the wood into the box behind the stove, grabbed the handle of the pan to move it to the sink, and realized as the heat burned his palm and fingers that he'd forgotten to use a towel or pot holder.

"Ouch!" He dropped the pan back on the stove, muttering darkly beneath his breath as he snagged a pot holder off a hook and moved the pan to the sink, where he filled it with water and then pushed open the window.

Frigid air stole into the room, but he hoped it would help the rancid smell of burned oatmeal dissipate in short order.

"Daddy? Did you get an owie?" Bodie asked, running into the room, then wrinkling his nose. "Something is stinky!"

"Yes, it is," Cord agreed as he ran cold water over his throbbing hand. "I burned my hand, but everything is fine. How about we go eat breakfast with Tug and the boys this morning?"

"Okay!" Bodie raced out of the room.

Cord shifted so he faced the doorway and raised his voice. "Go get dressed, son. Put on warm clothes and two pairs of socks."

"Aw, Daddy!" Bodie's voice carried back to him as the little boy's footsteps echoed down the hall and started up the stairs.

Cord hated cooking even more than he did trying to keep up the house. Both Filly and Ginny had offered to help him find a housekeeper or a cook, or both, but Cord had wanted to wait until after the holidays.

With oatmeal turning into a crisp, acrid mess on top of the stove and his palm already blistering from grabbing onto the hot handle of the pan, he concluded it was time to hire someone.

He had no idea who he could get, though. Ideally, whoever it was could both cook and clean, and, if he were making big wishes, they would keep an eye on Bodie while Cord worked. He still took his son with him all the time, unless Tug was available to watch him, but it wasn't exactly fair to Tug to leave Bodie with him often.

No, it was past time to hire some domestic help, but Cord had no idea where to even start. Cord's mother had seen to hiring help for his home in Boston. When he'd married Helen, she'd added a few more staff members.

He'd hired people for his banking office. Could the same principles apply to securing someone to help around the house?

Cord ran through a list of people who might offer suggestions but couldn't think of anyone in the community of Hardman who'd be available on short notice to take the position. Whoever he hired would need to be young enough to keep up with the demands of having a youngster in the house. Someone who could make Bodie mind while making him feel loved and valued was of the utmost importance to Cord, even more so than having a spotless house and a hot meal on the table at the end of the day.

As he thought about the qualifications of the position, a face popped into his mind—Gracy Randall.

Of course! It was the perfect solution to both his problem and hers. He needed a housekeeper and cook who could watch Bodie. She needed a job that would last more than a day or two.

The fact that Cord was attracted to her and felt some inexplicable pull to be near her didn't bear any significance on his sudden desire to hire her. Did it? No, it certainly did not. He was a business professional, and so was she. She'd worked for years for the Grass Valley telephone office, after all.

The two of them would just focus on their duties and nothing else. That's how it would have to be. Otherwise, gossiping tongues would start to wag. The last thing Cord wanted was for anything to tarnish Gracy's reputation. He wouldn't stand for it.

If she went home each evening before dark, there wouldn't be a reason for anyone to question what was going on out at Juniper Creek Ranch.

With plans rapidly forming, Cord left the oatmeal-scorched pan to soak in the sink, then went to help Bodie finish dressing. Once his son was bundled into his coat and boots, Cord pulled a knit stocking cap almost down to Bodie's cute little button nose.

"Daddy! That's not how it goes. I can't see!" Bodie protested, trying to shove at his cap with his mittened hands.

Cord chuckled and properly settled the hat on Bodie's head. He winked at his son, then held out his hand. "Are you ready for breakfast?"

"Yep! Let's go!" Bodie took his hand, and the two of them stepped outside into a nippy morning that promised to bring a beautiful day. Fresh snowfall covered every surface in a pristine layer of white. As the sun slowly began to rise, it would glisten over the world blanketed in white.

"Can we build a snowman, Daddy?"

"Maybe this afternoon, Bode. I may need to run into town this morning, but I'll talk to Tug first."

Bodie shrugged, as though it made no difference to him as they walked to the bunkhouse.

Cord tapped once on the door, then pushed it open, and Bodie skipped inside.

Tug stood at the stove, adding golden pancakes to a platter already stacked high. The scent of frying bacon mingled with coffee in the air.

"Do you have room for two more this morning?" Cord asked as Bodie yanked off his mittens and stocking cap.

"Sure, boss. Grub will be ready in about five minutes. You and Bodie can set the table if you like."

"Great," Cord said, then helped Bodie out of his coat and hung it with his on hooks by the door.

"Burn the oatmeal again?" Tug asked, offering Cord a knowing grin as he expertly flipped a pancake into the air, catching it in the pan.

"As a matter of fact, I did. The house smells like something crawled into the oven and died."

"There's dead things in our oven?" Bodie asked, giving Cord a wide-eyed look.

"No, son. It just smells that way. The only thing in the oven right now is air." Cord ruffled Bodie's hair, then took a stack of plates from a shelf and set them around the long table. He glanced over at Tug as he worked. "Would you have time to keep an eye on Bodie this morning? I'm going into town and hope to come back with a cook."

Tug turned around and gave him a long, observant look. "About time for that, I reckon. And the sprout can stay in here. I brought in some tack to repair this morning, and he can help with that."

"Thanks, Tug. I appreciate it." Cord knew how much the older man wanted to be working alongside the other cowboys on the ranch, but an injury to his knee two years ago kept him out of the saddle. The cold weather, especially, seemed to make it ache, so Tug stayed inside as much as possible and did what work he could from the barn or the bunkhouse. He could run the ranch with one eye closed and still do a better job than most men. Cord often sought Tug's advice or opinions before he made decisions because the old cowboy had many, many years of experience under his hat.

"You got someone in mind for the position?" Tug asked as he began forking bacon onto a platter.

"I do. Gracy Randall has been looking for work all over town. She and Bodie are no longer at war. I think she might work out well, especially since she's familiar with the ranch and the house."

Tug's bushy eyebrows shot upward toward his receding hairline. "Gracy, huh?"

Cord waited, expecting Tug to say more, but the man was as close-mouthed as a gambler with a losing hand. Unable to stand the silence, Cord glared at the older man. "Well? You have anything to say about that plan?"

"I think I'll just wait and see how that hand plays out for you." Tug grinned at him. "Gracy can be a mite of a handful, but I expect you already figured that out already. If that girl doesn't want the job, nothing you or anyone else says will convince her. If she decides it's a good idea, there isn't anything that will stand in her way of doing it and doing her very best at it. It's just the way she's always been. Gracy isn't one to do anything halfway."

"I see." Cord did see the wisdom in what Tug shared. He'd already seen Gracy's stubborn streak. But he'd also seen her kindness and her laughter. She and Bodie seemed to be getting along, and Cord had eaten at the Randall home with enough frequency to know Gracy could cook as well as her mother. In fact, there were a few things Cord thought she could make better, not that he'd ever share that opinion with anyone.

The ranch hands arrived for breakfast, faces and hands red from the cold, spurs jingling like sleigh bells as they teased and jostled each other on the way to the table. Cord burned meals with enough frequency that no one was surprised to see him or Bodie at the table. To a man, they all gave him polite nods or greetings.

Tug was the last to be seated, then he bowed his head and asked a blessing on the meal and each one gathered at the table.

"Amens!" Bodie said, joining his voice to the others and making Cord smile as the food was passed around the table.

After the meal was through, Tug gave each man his orders for the day. Cord sipped his coffee and added a few comments here and there, then nodded to the men as they left.

Once all the cowboys had returned outdoors, Cord finished his coffee and carried dishes to the sink while Tug washed them. When the table was cleared, Cord slipped on his coat, then lifted Bodie in his arms.

"I'm going to head into town for a while, Bodie. You stay here with Tug and mind what he tells you to do."

"I will, Daddy!" Bodie gave him a tight hug, kissed his cheek, then wiggled down. Since Bodie spent time in the bunkhouse, a box with a few toys, paper and pencils, and a blanket for naptime was kept beneath the bench by the front door. He reached for the box, but Cord nudged him toward the sink. "Why don't you help Tug dry the dishes, then you can play for a while."

"I get to help Tug?" Bodie asked, grabbing a chair and dragging it with a screech across the floor to the sink.

Tug winked at him and handed him a dish towel, then tipped his head to Cord. "Hope you have a successful hunting trip, boss."

"Me, too," Cord said, opening the door and stepping out into the cold.

He hated for anyone to come to his house and find the scorched oatmeal mess, so he returned to the house and cleaned it up. The kitchen no longer smelled atrocious, but the window he'd left open had made the house chilly. Cord shut the window, banked the stove and the fireplace in the front room, then spent a few minutes tidying the house. He made sure the bathroom was clean before he strode outside and went to the barn.

He debated riding his horse into town or taking the sleigh. If Gracy decided to come back with him, it would be better to take the sleigh, even if riding the horse would be faster.

Decision made, he harnessed a horse to the sleigh, waved to Bodie when he looked out the bunkhouse window, and headed into Hardman. The sleigh runners whooshed over the snow, and Cord found himself enjoying the trip. No one had yet been out on the road, so the journey made him feel like an explorer taking in a fresh world that had not yet been disturbed by human hands.

Cord went straight to the Randall home and hurried up the walk. He rang the bell and listened to approaching footsteps. The door swung open, and Gracy gave him a surprised look of welcome.

"Good morning," she said, moving back so he could enter, then looked behind him, as though she expected Bodie to bound into the house with his typical energy.

"Mornin', Gracy," he said, stepping inside and removing his hat. "Bodie is with Tug this morning."

"Oh," she said, closing the door and blocking out the cold that trailed him into the house. "Would you care for a cup of coffee or tea?"

"Tea would be nice," Cord said, unbuttoning his coat as he followed her down the hall to the kitchen.

The kitchen was tidy, and the breakfast dishes were already put away. Cord had expected to see Cleo there, but the house seemed quiet.

As though she sensed his thoughts, Gracy smiled at him as she lifted the kettle from the stovetop and poured a cup of steaming water. "Papa went to the newspaper office early, and Mama had a few errands to run before she attended the Christmas Carnival committee meeting. She's helping with the Christmas Eve celebration this year."

"She did mention that a while back," Cord said, standing with his hat in one hand and his coat in the other.

"Set your things down and have a seat," Gracy said as she made two cups of tea. "Have you eaten? I could make something for you, or we have crumb cake. Papa left behind a few pieces this morning."

"That was generous of him," Cord said in a wry tone, fully aware of how much Everett enjoyed cake for breakfast. "I wouldn't turn down a piece."

Gracy placed a square of cake on a plate and set it on the table along with the tea. Cord set his coat and hat on a chair, pulled out the one next to it for Gracy, then plunked into the seat across from her.

"Isn't it pretty outside this morning?" Gracy took a sip of hot tea as she gazed out the window. "It looks like a winter fairy waved a magic wand."

"I suppose it does," Cord said, amused by her fanciful way of describing the beauty of the morning.

Silence fell between them as Cord ate the moist, flavorful cake and sipped the hot tea with a hint of cinnamon to it. When he'd finished the last bite, Gracy cleared her throat.

"I assume you have a reason for dropping in, Cord. Is there something I can help you with today?"

Cord took a deep swig of tea and swallowed, then nodded his head. Apparently, Gracy was ready for answers to explain his unexpected arrival at the Randall home. "Have you found employment yet?"

Gracy shook her head. "No. If something doesn't present itself soon, I may be forced to leave. I know I could get work in a bigger town, especially one with a large telephone office. I hate to leave after just returning, but I can't expect my parents to take care of me forever when I could be earning my own way."

Cord nodded. "That's admirable and understandable. However, I don't think you'll have to pack up and leave Hardman anytime soon. I came this morning to offer you a job."

Gracy's face held a shocked expression, but she leaned forward. "Go on. What do you have in mind?"

"I need someone who can clean and cook and watch Bodie. I burned the oatmeal again this morning." He held out his hand, where three blisters dotted his palm. "Would you consider coming to work at the ranch?"

"I would consider it, but before I give you an answer, I'd like to discuss it with Mama and Papa. Are you in a rush? Were you planning on my starting today?" Gracy rose from the table and took a jar from a shelf near the sink. She resumed her seat, removed the lid, then reached across the table and took his hand in hers.

Cord felt a jolt that went from his fingers to his toes as she carefully rubbed ointment over his blisters, then wrapped a bit of gauze around his hand. She wiped her fingers on her napkin, returned the lid to the jar, and looked at him.

He realized he had yet to answer her questions. "I was hoping you might be willing to start today, but I would happily have you come whenever you are ready."

"You weren't expecting me to stay at the ranch, were you?"

"No," Cord shook his head, feeling a need to reassure her. "I know that would cause unnecessary gossip. I thought perhaps you could return home mid-afternoon each day, that way you'd be back here before dark."

Gracy nodded and appeared thoughtful, although she remained quiet for a time. Finally, she looked over at him, giving him a studying glance, as though searching for his true intentions. Cord had no hidden motives. He truly was in dire need of help at the house and with Bodie. It would just be an added bonus if the help were lovely Gracy Randall.

"Do you have errands you could see to this morning?" Gracy finally asked.

"Yes, I suppose there are some things to which I could attend." Cord drained his teacup and rose.

"Come back here for lunch, and I'll give you an answer. Will that be satisfactory?"

"Of course, Gracy. If you'd rather, I can come back tomorrow, or you could telephone once you decide."

She grinned at him. "Too many people listen on the telephone for me to have a conversation of any importance. I will give you my answer at noon."

"Fair enough. I'll be back then. Would you like to eat lunch out? I could take you to the bakery or the restaurant."

"That won't be necessary, but thank you for offering. I'll see you in a while." Gracy stood and handed him his coat and hat, then walked him to the door.

Cord shrugged into his coat and held his hat in one hand and the doorknob in the other. "I appreciate your even considering the possibility of helping me out, Gracy. Thank you."

"Of course, Cord." She smiled at him, and Cord fought the urge to kiss her right there in the entry. She looked like Christmas in a deep green skirt with green lace trimming the hem and a green and red plaid shirtwaist with tiny green buttons marching down the front of it.

He gave her a parting nod, then hurried out to the sleigh.

Cord had no idea what he'd do for the next three and a half hours but realized he had yet to purchase any gifts for Christmas, and the holiday was only a week away. He headed to the Bruner's mercantile and leisurely browsed up and down each aisle, thinking of people for whom he should purchase gifts.

"Good morning, Cord. May I assist you with anything this morning?" Aleta Bruner asked as she noticed him lingering near a display of leather work gloves.

"I need to do some Christmas shopping. Do you think you could wrap everything for me?"

Aleta smiled. "Of course. You just tell me what you have in mind, and I'll do my best to take care of it."

"Let's start with gloves for all my ranch hands. I'll need eight pairs. I'll need about two dozen Christmas greeting cards too. I'm also looking for gifts for my sister and her family, my cousins, the Randalls, and ..."

Aleta held up a hand, then slid a pad of paper and a pencil toward him. "Why don't you start a list while I go in the back and get the gloves?"

Cord jotted down a list of names and then the ideas he had for gifts. Aleta spent an hour helping him choose items. While she wrapped everything, he walked over to the Rutherfords' bookstore. He selected storybooks for Bodie and Patrick, and books for Cullen, Maura, Seth, and Judd, as well as his sister and her family.

A stationery set of green vines on a fine parchment background made him think of Gracy, so he added it to the pile of gifts.

"Anything else?" Brynn Bruner asked as she rang up his purchases.

"That should do it. Do you offer gift wrapping services?"

Brynn grinned at him. "I certainly do. Just write for whom each book is intended and I'll make sure they have a tag on them."

"Thank you, Brynn. That's most helpful." Cord wrote the name for each book, and then looked at the gifts for his sister. He hoped if he got them in the mail today, they'd arrive in time for Christmas. He had a few more things he wanted to get, then he could box up everything and get it on its way. Aleta had offered to provide a box for him, and he'd thanked her for her help.

"If you come back in about an hour, I'll have everything ready." Brynn handed him his change and picked up the tall stack of books, moving them to the counter behind her.

"Great. Thank you." Cord tipped his head to her, then hurried outside. He saw Gracy standing outside the newspaper office deep in conversation with her father but didn't disturb them.

Instead, he visited the saddle maker and the blacksmith shop, then stopped at the bakery and bought several boxes full of treats.

After a glance at his watch, he went to the post office to collect his mail, stopped back by the bookstore and gathered his purchases from Brynn, then returned to Bruner's Mercantile.

Aleta helped him box up the gifts for Cornelia and even offered to ship it for him. Cord took her up on the generous offer, leaving a hefty tip with the money to pay the shipping expense, then loaded his purchases in the sleigh.

It was five minutes before noon when he pulled the sleigh to a stop in front of the Randall home.

With a box of cinnamon buns from the bakery in hand, he walked up the porch steps and rang the bell.

The door swung open almost immediately, as though Gracy had been watching for him.

"You're right on time," she said, welcoming him inside for the second time that day.

"I brought some of Elsa's cinnamon buns." Cord handed the box to her, then removed his hat and coat, leaving them by the door.

"Thank you. They are so delicious. They'll taste wonderful with a cup of coffee later."

Cord nodded and followed her back to the kitchen, where the aromas of meat and something yeasty hung in the air. His stomach growled, and he realized he was hungry despite his filling breakfast and the cake Gracy had served to him earlier.

The food was on the table, so Cord quickly washed his hands, pulled out a chair for Gracy, and took a seat across from her. She glanced at him, then bowed her head and asked a blessing on the meal.

"Thank you for making lunch, Gracy. I would have happily taken you somewhere so you didn't have to cook." Cord draped the napkin over his lap and glanced down at the bowl of thick soup sitting in front of him. Chunks of beef, potatoes, and vegetables were coated in what looked like a rich gravy. Gracy had placed two slices of bread still warm from the oven on his plate. Butter melted into every crevice, and there were two dishes of jam to choose from on the table.

"I hope you like it. I was going to make the soup for lunch anyway. Mama decided to eat with one of her friends at the restaurant, and Papa took a sandwich with him this morning. There's nothing like a bowl of soup on a snowy day."

"Or warm bread," Cord said, dunking a corner of the bread into his soup and relishing the bite. "So good."

While they ate, they discussed the upcoming Christmas Eve program at church, the holiday event planned at his aunt Dora's home and other festivities around town.

"Does Bodie have his costume for the Christmas Eve program?" Gracy asked as Cord used the last bite of his bread to sop up the remaining bit of broth in his soup bowl.

"Costume? He needs a costume?" Had Cord somehow missed that detail?

"He is in the pageant, isn't he?" Gracy asked, wiping her mouth on her napkin and leaning back in her chair. "I thought I saw him with the children who were practicing after church on Sunday."

"He was, he is." Cord sighed. "I think I overlooked the costume part of his involvement, though."

"What part is he playing?" Gracy questioned.

Cord had been so busy studying the way sunlight had set Gracy's hair aflame as she'd sat in the pew in front of him and Bodie, he'd hardly paid any attention to the service, let alone the parts that were assigned to the children.

When Cord remained silent, Gracy gave him a reproachful look. "I'll ask Brynn. She and Percy are in charge of the program this year."

"Thank you." Cord felt tense as he waited to broach the real reason he was there.

Gracy rose from the table and carried his dishes to the sink, then returned with a bowl of creamy vanilla pudding that was still warm. She added a dollop of berry jam to the top before setting it in front of him.

SHANNA HATFIELD

"This looks wonderful." Cord waited until she picked up her spoon to dig into the pudding. "Mmm. Don't tell your mother, but this is even better than her chocolate pudding."

"I won't say a word," Gracy said, appearing pleased by his praise. "I thought we should eat lunch here so you could sample my cooking. If I'm going to work as your cook, I thought you should know what you're getting. I know you've eaten my cooking before, but you probably didn't know what I made or what Mama made since we often cook together."

"I had a few ideas, but I knew enough to realize you're a good cook, Gracy." He grinned at her as he spooned another bite of pudding. "Does this mean you're considering my job offer?"

"I have considered it. Prayed about it. Discussed it with both Mama and Papa." Gracy looked across the table at him and set down her spoon. "What I propose is working for you on a temporary basis, just to see if all parties involved are pleased with the arrangement. I thought by Christmas we'd know if we should continue or if you should find someone else for the position. Would that be satisfactory?"

Cord frowned. "That's fine, Gracy, but I already know you'll do a great job as a cook and taking care of the house. I saw the other day how good you are with Bodie. He couldn't stop talking about how much fun he had with you baking cookies and sledding."

"I'm glad he had a grand time. I did as well. However, in light of our first meeting at the ranch, I

178

just thought we might ease into the idea of my being there on a more permanent basis. If Bodie isn't happy with the arrangement, then I will seek employment elsewhere."

Cord wanted to assure her his son would be thrilled with her presence there every day, but he couldn't state what he didn't know for a fact. He thought Bodie would be happy to have Gracy come each day, but until he knew for certain, he decided to agree with Gracy's plan. It was reasonable and made sense.

"That's fair, Gracy. What hours would you plan to be at the house?"

"I could arrive no later than half past eight each morning and stay until half past three. That way I wouldn't travel in the dark either coming or going. I'll plan to cook lunch, and leave something on the stove for dinner. I would expect to have Sundays off. Will that work for you, Cord?"

"Yes, of course. I could come and get you each day and bring you home," he offered.

Gracy shook her head. "No. That won't be necessary. I'll just ride Cider out. If she can stay in your barn during the day, I see no reason to plan on anything different."

"All right, then. Would you like to start tomorrow?"

Gracy shrugged. "I thought perhaps I could go out this afternoon and ease Bodie into the idea of my being there if that suits you."

Cord fought the urge to stand up and cheer. "Yes, that suits me fine. Why don't you just ride with me in the sleigh, and I'll bring you back later this afternoon."

"Very well. You and Bodie can plan on staying for supper with us then."

Cord smirked at her. "You drive a hard bargain, Miss Randall."

She laughed, and the sound of it winged its way straight into his heart. He rubbed his chest, amazed that he was feeling something besides grief. Truthfully, Gracy made him feel far more than he wanted to, but now was not the time to examine his feelings when it came to the intriguing woman. She could be cool and reserved one moment and brimming with laughter and joy the next. He wondered, given a lifetime to unravel the mystery of her, if he'd make it past the outermost layers.

Rather than further examine the possibilities, he finished his pudding, then rose and helped Gracy with the dishes.

"Do you or your mother have anything planned for supper?"

"Nothing in particular," Gracy said as she rinsed the last dish, and he took it from her, wiping it dry.

"Why don't I treat you all to dinner out tonight? Your mother has fed Bodie and me more times than I can count. It would be such a little thing to do in thanks for all the meals we've shared around the Randall table."

"If Mama and Papa don't mind, I'm agreeable to your suggestion. I'll leave them a note in case they return home before we arrive." Gracy wrote a note and left it on the counter, then gathered her coat and scarf from near the back door.

While she pulled on her boots, Cord banked the fire in the fireplace and the kitchen stove, then held her coat as she slipped it on. She wrapped a thick scarf around her head, ears, and neck, then pulled on a pair of fur-lined mittens.

Cord opened the door, and she preceded him out to the sleigh. He wanted to span her slender waist and lift her into it, but he instead held out a hand.

She placed hers on it and stepped into the sleigh with grace, settling her skirts around her.

Cord hurried around and climbed in on the other side, wondering what she'd do if he leaned over and kissed her.

A vision of her slugging him in the nose or blackening his eye made him work to hide a grin as he snapped the lines and the sleigh started down the street.

Chapter Twelve

"Do you have any Christmas decorations, Bodie?" Gracy asked as she dusted the baseboards in the upstairs hallway in the house that had once been her home.

Bodie shrugged and pushed a toy wooden horse across the floor.

"What's your horse's name?" Gracy asked as she worked.

Bodie held the horse up and turned to her. "Mup."

"Mup?"

"Uh, huh." Bodie returned to quietly playing with the horse.

Gracy wondered if he and the horse galloped across an open prairie or over mountain ridges in his imagination. She straightened and stretched her back, then ran a dust cloth over a painting of a sunny garden filled with colorful flowers, admiring the beauty of it before she again bent down to dust the baseboards.

"What's that?" Bodie asked, pointing to the doorframe outside the bedroom that had once been Gracy's.

Gracy dropped down to her knees beside him, settled an arm around him, and pointed to a line with writing beside it.

"Gracy. Age five," she read, then noted the date. During her growing up years, her father had measured her height on the first day of January and the first day of summer. "My papa made these marks to show how much I grew each year."

Bodie cocked his head and looked at her, then at the lines. "You used to be short."

She laughed. "I suppose I was, but once I was the same size as you."

His eyes widened. "You were?"

"I was. And then I grew and grew." Gracy's fingers traced the lines as they moved higher on the doorframe.

"Wait here!" Brody hopped to his feet and raced down the stairs. She heard him run down the hallway, and his steps grew louder as he returned. He topped the stairs with a pencil held tightly in his fist. "Do me, Gracy! Please? Show how much I grow! Please?"

"Sure, Bodie." Gracy took the pencil from his hand and guided him to stand with his heels and head against the doorframe.

The little boy acted like he had ants in his pants for as much as he squirmed with excitement. "Are you done?"

"You have to hold still, Bodie," Gracy instructed, bending over and planting her tongue in cheek as she drew a line above Bodie's head with the pencil.

"Can I see now?" he asked, unable to keep his wiggly body from moving.

Gracy wrote his age and the date on the doorframe and nodded. "You may look."

Bodie spun around and looked where she pointed to the mark on the opposite side of the doorframe from where her father had made the marks to chart her growth.

"That's you, right there," Gracy said, showing him the line she'd just made.

Bodie traced the line with his index finger, then he looked at the marks from her childhood. "Where's your line, like mine?"

"You mean when I was your age?" Gracy asked, guiding his finger to the line made in January when she was five. "This is how tall I was when I was close to your age."

Bodie grinned. "I'm taller!"

"Yes, you are, but you're a big boy like your daddy, aren't you?" Gracy had earlier dusted a photo in Bodie's room of Cord with a delicate-appearing woman who held an infant Bodie in her arms. She looked so frail and petite, it was clear

Bodie got his size from his father and not his mother.

"I'm a big boy!" Bodie said, puffing out his little chest and strutting in a circle, making Gracy laugh.

She stepped into the bedroom that had once been hers, recalling so many happy memories spent there as a child.

She'd loved the room then but had to admit it was quite lovely with the golden oak bedroom set and the beautiful coverlet with yellow and blue flowers embroidered across the top like wildflowers that had been scattered in the snow.

Gracy moved over to the window and looked outside. Cord and three of the hired hands were working to repair a fence the cattle had plowed through during the night. She'd arrived this morning, her second day on the job, to find cows bellowing, calves bawling, men shouting, and Bodie in the bunkhouse with Tug, who was grousing about not being able to mount up and help get the disgruntled bovines rounded up and back where they belonged.

Cord seemed to think a mountain lion may have spooked the cattle and sent them racing through the fence.

At any rate, repairs were needed, and they'd been at it most of the morning.

Bodie had been more than happy to return to the house with Gracy, and she'd rushed to fix a hearty stew to simmer for lunch, baked a batch of sugar cookies, and then started cleaning. She thought it best to begin upstairs and work her way down.

Much to her delight, Bodie's room was tidy, just in need of a good dusting. The little boy wanted to help, so she gave him a dust cloth, and he attempted to wipe off his toys while she took care of dusting the furniture and the low shelves that held an assortment of storybooks.

Now, as she stood in her old bedroom, she felt a yearning to be out in the fresh air, but it was far too cold for Bodie to be out for long, and there was plenty to keep them busy in the house.

She was disturbed to see not a single Christmas decoration or festive bit of cheer in the house. Luke and Filly Granger always had decorations both inside and out at their house. She couldn't imagine Cord wouldn't do anything to mark the holiday for his son. Perhaps he'd merely forgotten about decorating.

Or perhaps he didn't have any decorations. Her mother had mentioned he'd left behind many things in Boston that he couldn't bear to see because they reminded him of his wife. Maybe he'd left all the trappings of Christmas there as well.

Gracy was musing over the possibilities as she returned to dusting. Bodie alternated between flapping his dust rag around and playing with Mup. Gracy intended to ask Cord about the toy's odd name when she had a moment.

She and Bodie finished cleaning upstairs and returned to the kitchen, where Gracy made a big pan of cornbread, then fried two apples in a pan of hot butter with a sprinkling of sugar on top.

"Boy, something smells good," Cord called as he stepped inside the house through the back door.

A draft of cold air blew in around him, but Gracy smiled at the sound of his spurs jangling.

"Daddy!" Bodie exclaimed, running to greet him.

Cord stepped into the kitchen with his son in his arms and a smile on his handsome face. "This is a nice way to come in out of the cold. A son happy to see me, the house filled with delicious aromas, and a pretty woman in my kitchen."

Gracy blushed, then shook the spoon she held at him. "You'd best behave yourself, Mr. Granger, or you'll find yourself without two of the three things you just listed."

Cord winked at her, set Bodie on his feet, then toed off his boots and left them with his coat by the back door. He disappeared down the hall, and she heard water running in the bathroom.

He returned with his hair combed back and his hands and face clean.

"Daddy, come upstairs. I gots to show you what me and Gracy did!"

Cord gave her a questioning look but allowed Bodie to pull him from the kitchen.

She could hear the resonant tone of Cord's voice and the hum of Bodie's as he excitedly led his father upstairs to see the mark on the doorframe.

Cord returned with Bodie riding on his back and deposited his son in his chair at the table. "Thank you for doing that, Gracy. I've thought about marking his height a dozen times and always forget."

"You're welcome. And before I forget, I wanted to ask if you have any Christmas decorations. I'd be happy to set them out for you."

"Thank you. There's a trunk full of them in the attic. I can haul it down for you. I intend to go with Luke and Blake to get a t-r-e-e in a few days. One of the boxes in the trunk has ornaments."

Bodie pointed to Cord. "When you spell words, I know you don't want me to know stuff."

"That's right. When you learn how to spell, then I'll be in trouble, won't I?" Cord asked, tweaking his son's nose.

Bodie giggled. "You're in trouble now."

"I am?"

"Yes!" Bodie's giggles turned into belly laughs as Cord tickled his sides, then kissed the top of his head.

"Are you two ready for lunch?" Gracy asked as she brought bowls of stew to the table, a bowl with the fried apples, and a plate full of cornbread.

Cord hurried to pull out a chair for her and took a seat across the table, so Bodie sat between them. Bodie reached out a hand to each of them. When Gracy stretched out her hand to connect with his, she could see Cord bowing his head to hide a smile. The three of them sitting there, joined together by hands and hearts, felt so perfect, so right. It took her so far aback, she missed half of what Bodie said as he offered a simple prayer.

"Amens!" Bodie said enthusiastically, then tucked his napkin into the front of his shirt.

"Do yours like mine, Daddy!" Bodie said, grabbing the napkin off Cord's lap and attempting to stuff it in his shirt.

Cord looked at Gracy, and she shrugged, unable to keep the humor from dancing in her eyes. To please his son, Cord tucked the napkin into the front of his shirt and reached for his soup spoon.

"You too, Gracy," Bodie said, stretching out his arm to reach for her napkin.

"Now, son," Cord said, shaking his head at Bodie, "ladies don't tuck their napkins into their shirts like boys do."

"That's right, Bodie," Gracy said, smiling at the little boy. "If they aren't across our laps, should we wear them on our heads?" She dropped the napkin on top of her head, crossed her eyes, and made a silly face that caused Bodie to giggle and Cord to chuckle.

"That's not how it goes, Gracy!" Bodie sat on his knees in the chair and leaned toward her. He lost his balance and started to fall, but Gracy pulled him onto her lap, then smothered his cheeks with kisses, making him laugh.

"Stop, Gracy. Stop!" Bodie made no effort to get away from her, though. In fact, he gave her a tight hug, then kissed her cheek before he hopped off her lap and climbed back onto his chair. He still held her napkin, so he tossed it at her.

Gracy once again draped it across her lap, then winked at Bodie. She had no idea what Cord thought of her being playful with Bodie, but he didn't seem concerned as he buttered cornbread and spread honey across it, then busied himself with his meal.

She served cookies and canned peaches for dessert. Bodie ate two cookies, drained his glass of milk, then asked to be excused.

"He likes to sit by the fire after lunch, and I read to him. Most of the time, he falls asleep for an hour or so," Cord said quietly as Bodie skipped out of the room and down the hall.

"By all means, keep his routine. I'll just clean up from lunch while you do." Gracy already had her hands in a pan of hot dishwater and soap up to her wrists.

"Everything was delicious, Gracy. Thank you for a fine meal and for taking such good care of my son."

Cord kissed her cheek, and Gracy was certain sparks snapped in the air around them. She nodded her head, unable to speak for fear she'd say something to embarrass herself, like asking Cord to kiss her again, or maybe hold her close in those strong arms.

What was she doing, thinking in terms of romance where Cord Granger was concerned? Now that he was her employer she absolutely couldn't or wouldn't allow herself to fall in love.

If she were being honest with herself, she'd admit she was already half in love with the man. He was kind and caring, funny and gentle, a wonderful father, and a good friend. He was intelligent and so interesting to talk to, but he also was a good listener. Her parents thought he was fantastic, but nothing could ever happen between her and Cord.

He came from money, and she didn't. She would never be a fine lady like his first wife had been. There was no possibility she could ever fill Helen's expensive shoes.

Besides, Gracy was at the ranch to work and nothing more. She could cook and clean and care for Bodie, and anything more than that was only a disappointment if she allowed it to be.

Determined not to let Cord turn her head any more than he'd already done, she finished the dishes, set a roast in the oven to cook with carrots and potatoes, and whipped up a gingerbread cake for dessert. While the cake baked, she went to the front room to find both Cord and Bodie asleep in the rocking chair by the fire.

According to Tug, Cord had been up since five chasing the cows. He was probably exhausted. Afraid to wake either of them, Gracy backed from the room and returned to the kitchen, where she scrubbed the insides of the windows. She removed the cake from the oven and turned to place it on the counter to cool only to find Cord watching her.

His hair was tousled, and he had a sleepy look in his eyes that made heat swirl through her extremities. He gave her a lazy smile that threatened to weaken her knees.

For a moment she pondered what it would be like to wake every morning to that smile, that face, those eyes full of warmth and affection.

Ridiculous! she chastised herself, then set the cake down and moved to the stove. "Would you like some coffee?"

"If you have some ready. If not, I should probably head back out. The guys are most likely wondering if I got lost on my way back to the barn after lunch."

Gracy grinned and handed him a cup of hot coffee. "I'll be sure to tell them you needed a nap today."

Cord scowled at her as he blew on the steaming brew. "You'll do no such thing, miss smarty. I work hard to earn a little respect around this place and don't need you destroying it the first few days you're here."

"Fine. I'll keep your nap to myself. I put a roast in the oven for your supper. All you need to do is take it out and cut the meat when you're ready to eat. I'll frost the cake and leave it under a clean towel on the counter. There are biscuits in that tin there," she pointed to a large tin on the counter. "If you want another vegetable for dinner, I can set out a jar of peas."

"That won't be necessary, but thank you." Cord hurriedly drank his coffee, handed her the cup, then kissed her cheek. "If I don't see you before you leave today, thank you for everything you've done already."

"My pleasure, Cord. It's nice to feel useful."

He gave her a look she hesitated to interpret, then hurried into the hallway. She heard him tamp on his boots and then open the door. A blast of cold air circled into the kitchen before he could close the door.

Gracy leaned forward and watched out the window as he pulled on his coat on his way to the barn.

How was she supposed to keep her attraction to Cord Granger from growing when he did things like kiss her cheek and thank her for every little thing?

Determined to take her emotions in hand, Gracy returned to cleaning, realizing only after she finished dusting the dining room that Cord had forgotten to bring down the Christmas decorations.

SHANNA HATFIELD

Chapter Thirteen

"What is that thing?" Cord asked, hesitant to accept the big ball of greens that Luke held out to him by a bright red bow.

"A Christmas decoration. According to Maura, you need some holiday cheer at your house. She made this for you last night and asked me to give it to you when you came into town today. It was a good thing you called yesterday and said you'd be dropping by." Luke dangled the kissing ball from his finger. "You aren't planning to insult my little girl and refuse to hang this at your house, are you?"

Cord growled at Luke, but took the ball from him, holding it out like a poisonous spider lurked inside the greens, waiting to attack. He recognized mistletoe among the evergreen branches and bits of holly tucked in here and there, along with a few silk flowers. A fluffy red bow with a loop for hanging was fastened at the top of the ball. If what it represented didn't annoy him so greatly, he might have thought it was pretty.

However, the last thing he needed was a kissing ball hanging in his home when he could barely keep his thoughts—and lips—off Gracy as it was.

He released a resigned sigh. "Tell Maura I said it's much appreciated."

Luke smirked. "I can send her to your place after school to help you hang it."

"That won't be necessary, but thank you for that generous offer." Cord set the ball on the corner of Luke's desk, then took an envelope from his coat pocket. "I need to make a withdrawal."

"You mentioned that on the telephone yesterday. What do you need?" Luke switched from tormenting cousin mode into banker mode.

Cord wanted to give cash bonuses to his hired hands and planned to tuck the money into the Christmas greeting cards he'd purchased from Aleta along with a note thanking each man for his hard work all year. He gave Luke the total he wanted for each of the cowboys in his employ.

"You do know those bonuses are generous, don't you?" Luke asked as he counted out the cash.

"I do, but they've more than earned it." Cord glanced around the bank and nodded at Arlan Guthry as he waited on a customer. "Did the thing I bought for Bodie arrive?"

"Yep. Came in with the freight wagon yesterday. It's out in my barn along with Patrick's gift. I'm gonna be hard-pressed to keep my nosy offspring from finding their gifts before Christmas."

Cord chuckled. "Haven't you told them Saint Nicholas won't visit if they don't mind their manners?"

"Oh, I've used every threat my parents ever tossed at me, and several I made up. The problem is they take after their mother and are twice as smart as me, and they seem to have an innate ability to know when I'm trying to pull the wool over their eyes."

Cord chuckled. "Well, I'll wish you luck. It's only three more days until Christmas, so hopefully, they'll behave until then."

"I hope so," Luke said, counting out the last of the money and handing it to Cord. "How are things going with your newly hired help? Does she get a bonus too? Maybe some jewelry, like a gold band?"

Cord glowered at Luke as he tucked the money into the envelope he'd brought along and stuffed it into his pocket.

"Gracy is my housekeeper and cook, and she takes care of Bodie. That's it. There is no budding romance or anything else going on."

Luke held up his hands, as though warding off an attack. "Don't get so worked up, Cord. I'm just teasing. Is there something you want to talk about?"

"No!" Cord snapped, then lowered his voice when both Arlan and the customer glared at him. "Maybe."

Luke handed Cord the kissing ball, nudged him toward the door, and grabbed his coat on their way outside. "I'll be back in a few minutes, Arlan," he called over his shoulder, then followed Cord out into the morning chill. "Let's take a walk."

"A walk? It's freezing out here." Cord had no intentions of going for a walk or telling Luke what was on his mind. Before he could stop himself, though, his thoughts began spilling out of his mouth. "Gracy is incredible and beautiful, smart and feisty, and nothing like Helen. Not a single thing like her. Helen always bowed to my wishes, never argued, was always so meek and quiet, but Gracy will just tilt that stubborn chin and tell me exactly what she thinks about something. She's amazing with Bodie and a great cook, and the house has never looked better. She's not afraid to get dirty, and she works so hard. Gracy is vibrant and mysterious and nothing like I'd imagined after our first rather testy encounter. She's … Gracy."

"Yes, she is." Luke gave him an observant look. "You know you don't have to compare her to Helen, don't you? I agree the difference in the two women is like night and day, but I think Helen would want you to be happy again, Cord. She'd want you to know love again. Helen would have approved of Gracy, not because the two of them are so different, but because Gracy is a good person who makes you laugh, and she loves Bodie."

Cord couldn't speak past the emotion that suddenly clogged his throat. He set his gaze on a point in the distance and willed himself to gain control of the turmoil simmering beneath the surface.

Luke stopped and placed a hand on his shoulder, giving it a comforting squeeze. "It's okay to grieve, Cord, and it's okay to be sad sometimes. Mourn Helen for as long as you need to, but don't use your grief as an excuse to hide from life. There's not a thing wrong with your falling in love again or claiming all the happiness you can find. Life's too short, far too short, to be anything but happy. It seems to me you've been happier these last few weeks since Gracy's been back in Hardman than I've seen you for a long time, maybe ever."

Cord nodded, letting Luke's words sink in. He did care for Gracy. In fact, he knew he'd fallen in love with her, but it still seemed too soon. Their relationship was too new to take that next step. At least that was what he kept telling himself. Gracy fit so perfectly into his life and at the ranch.

Then again, the ranch had been her home until she'd left nearly six years ago. She knew every square inch of it and had even made some helpful suggestions to him in the days she'd worked there. She seemed to enjoy spending time with Tug, well acquainted with the old cowboy from her growing-up years.

If Cord could choose a woman to be his wife and partner in life, he couldn't picture anyone better than Gracy to fill the position or his arms. She would never meekly tiptoe around him, seeing to his every wish and whim, but she would challenge him, bring out the best in him, and fill his days with both fun and frustration.

Cord looked forward to her arrival each morning and hated returning in the afternoons to find her gone. Each afternoon at half past three, she took Bodie out to the bunkhouse to stay with Tug until Cord returned from whatever he was doing.

Twice, Cord had hurried to get back to the house before she left, but she'd already gone. Part of him wondered if she made certain she was headed back to town before he returned to avoid saying goodbye because she didn't like to say it either. Or perhaps he'd imagined her interest in him, and his feelings were unreturned.

The only way to know for sure, to know if she cared for him, was to ask, but he was afraid to do that. To bare his heart and soul to another, especially when Gracy held the power to wound him deeply due to his burgeoning affection for her, proved a challenge he wasn't sure he could conquer. At least not now.

Maybe after another month or two, when they'd had time to get to know one another better, he might ask to court her. Of course, he'd have to find someone else to keep house and cook for him. He certainly couldn't court Gracy while she was working for him.

In that moment, the entire situation seemed far too complicated to sort out, especially with Christmas so near.

"Just give some thought to what I said, cousin. If you ever want to talk, you know I'm here." Luke patted him on the shoulder, then turned around and walked back to the bank.

Cord glanced down at the kissing ball still dangling from his gloved finger, rolled his eyes heavenward, and headed for the sleigh he'd parked by the mercantile.

He set the kissing ball in the sleigh, finished the errands that had sent him to town, then headed back out to the ranch. After he saw to the horse and made sure the sleigh was under the cover of the carriage house to keep it dry, he carried a large box of supplies to the house with the stupid kissing ball bouncing around on top.

When Cord entered the house, the smell of peppermint filled the air and made his mouth water.

"Daddy! We made cookies!" Bodie shouted as he raced down the hallway and greeted Cord with an enthusiastic hug. The little boy had crumbs around one corner of his mouth as he offered a happy smile, and the sight of it warmed Cord's heart. Gracy was the reason for it. Cord had noticed Bodie seemed more settled and less likely to get into trouble now that Gracy was there every day. Perhaps his son's misbehavior had stemmed from a need for disciplined attention.

Cord knew Gracy didn't allow Bodie to get away with anything he shouldn't, but she also made opportunities for fun and learning throughout the day.

The look on Bodie's face, eager for Cord's approval, drew him back to the moment.

"Cookies? Who likes cookies?" Cord asked, setting the box of things he carried on the bench by the back door. He stuffed his gloves into his coat pockets, removed his hat and coat, and hung them on the hooks by the back door.

"We do!" Bodie grabbed his hand and tugged him into the kitchen, where Gracy stood at the stove stirring what appeared to be a pan of gravy.

"You're right on time for lunch," she said, looking up and smiling at him. The heat from the stove had given her face a pink flush that was almost as becoming as the tendrils of hair that framed her face. Flour dusted the tip of her nose, and splatters of gravy dotted the front of her apron, but Cord thought she looked entirely enchanting.

He took three steps in her direction before he stopped himself and turned to the sink. Maybe washing his hands would give him time to gather enough of his scattered wits together so he wouldn't do something foolhardy like sweep Gracy into his arms and lavish her with kisses.

The entire trip home, he'd done nothing but mull over Luke's words. He knew Helen would want him to love again. He also knew she would have liked Gracy because she was full of pluck and spunk, but especially because she'd brought laughter and joy back into his and Bodie's world.

Gracy was nothing like Cord had ever imagined a woman in his life would be, but his life had taken so many turns and new roads, it looked nothing like he'd planned when he'd been fresh out of school and full of dreams.

Cord concluded the best thing to do would be to set aside his feelings, for now, get through the holiday season, and then cautiously go about introducing the idea of a courtship to Gracy.

He had a feeling that if he asked her today to allow him to court her, she'd flat-out refuse without even blinking an eye.

Unaware of his change in expression, he scowled.

"Do you have indigestion, or is something wrong?" Gracy teased as she carried a bowl of mashed potatoes to the table.

"I'm fine," Cord said curtly.

She gave him an observant glance, then that stubborn chin tilted upward ever so slightly. "Really, Cord? Generally, when people are as snappish as you are and their forehead's furrowed like a plowed field, something is definitely wrong. If you keep making faces like that, someone might mistake you for a rabid dog and put you out of your misery. Who stuffed a burr under your blanket while you were in town?"

Rather than answer her question, he returned the cool glare she lobbed at him. "I'm not the only one who sounds a bit peevish. I've seen riled bees in better humor than you are at the moment." Cord knew it was crazy, but the more they sparred verbally, the greater he enjoyed it. She'd called him a name yesterday that had caused him to spend ten minutes trying to find it in the dictionary last night after he'd tucked Bodie into bed. He wasn't accustomed to any female interacting with him in such a manner and found he quite enjoyed it when Gracy stood toe to toe with him, at least on an intellectual level.

He assumed if she ever got close enough for their toes to touch, he'd lose every last bit of restraint he possessed and kiss her like he'd been dreaming of doing for weeks.

In fact, Cord felt as though he'd been walking around in a dazed fog since Gracy had caught his eye. At night, he tossed and turned, unable to sleep, with thoughts of her infiltrating his dreams. In the day, having her at the ranch made it doubly hard to pretend she was nothing more than a friend he'd hired to help him out with the house and Bodie.

The truth of the matter was that Cord could hardly corral his thoughts long enough to get them off Gracy. He'd found himself watching for her as he worked, hoping for a glimpse of that red hair or a swish of her skirt, or the sound of her laughter floating on the frosty December air.

Perhaps Luke was right when he'd told him that the last spill he'd taken off a bucking bronc had addled his brains. They felt more like Tug's scrambled eggs now than anything that could help him make sense of his current situation.

A voice in the back of his head whispered *Would it be so hard to love Gracy?* but Cord refused to answer it or acknowledge it. From the day she'd marched up the lane and demanded to know where her parents were, she'd turned his world upside down and left him feeling like he'd been sucked into the center of a hurricane, uncertain which way was up or down.

One moment she was feisty and full of sass, and in the next, she'd look at him with warmth in those pretty blue eyes that made him feel like he was playing with fire.

Cord felt himself falling into their depths even as she continued to glare at him, holding the gravy boat as though she was considering pouring it over his head.

"Daddy! What's a rabbit dog? Does he chase rabbits? Do you have a rabbit?" Bodie asked, patting Cord on the thigh to make sure he had his attention.

"I don't have a rabbit or a rabbit dog, son, but I think we might have a sly fox in our midst, one with beautiful red hair and a sweet smile." He grinned at Gracy and was gratified to see her looking at him in surprise. When she remained halfway across the kitchen, standing with the gravy boat in hand, he took it from her, set it on the table, then swung Bodie into his chair.

"Everything looks great, Gracy," he said, setting a plate of fried steaks on the table, then pouring milk for all three of them.

Gracy finally seemed to grasp onto her senses and rushed to set a bowl of buttered corn and a dish of strawberry jam on the table before plopping into her seat.

"Bodie, how about you give thanks for our meal?" Cord asked as he took a seat beside his son.

Bodie nodded so vigorously, his bangs flopped forward, but he bowed his head and steepled his little fingers together.

The childish prayer, offered in simple humility and sincerity, touched Cord's heart. Then Bodie finished with, "and thank you for sending us Gracy so we can have good things to eat and I can have someone who sings to me and bakes cookies and smells nice, just like a mama should. Amens!"

Cord lifted his head as Bodie started to hum, eager for the meal and completely unaware of how his words had affected his father. Cord's gaze drifted over to Gracy. She appeared contemplative as she spooned mashed potatoes onto Bodie's plate.

When she looked over at him, her expression appeared apologetic, as though Bodie's mention of her doing things like a mother would upset him. He did feel … Cord wasn't sure what he felt. He wasn't angry. He wasn't disappointed. He wasn't exactly pleased, though. But that might be due to the fact that he felt he was failing his son more than anything Gracy had done.

In all honesty, she'd been a huge blessing to him. She cooked a delicious, filling lunch each day and left an equally tasty dinner in the oven for him to enjoy for supper. She'd cleaned every room from top to bottom, and just her presence there had made the house finally feel like home. Gracy had done the laundry, washed the windows, and showered Bodie with love, which was something so priceless, Cord couldn't begin to imagine how he'd ever compensate her for that.

Luke's teasing about giving her a bonus trickled through his mind. He wasn't ready to give her a ring or propose, but Gracy deserved more than just the wage he'd offered to pay her. However, he didn't think she came and worked so hard every day for the money.

He could see how much she loved being out at the ranch and in the house that had been her childhood home. One morning, she'd tracked him down as he'd worked in the equipment shed and asked if he'd mind if she took Bodie for a ride on Cider around the ranch. He'd seen her ride enough to know she could be trusted with such precious cargo, so he agreed.

Bodie had still been excitedly recalling details of the ride when Cord had tucked him into bed that night.

As he buttered a soft roll and set it on Bodie's plate, he realized Gracy had not only filled the role of "just like a mama should," as Bodie had stated, but she'd also stood in the gap for things he'd neglected or not realized he should be doing for his son, like giving him the simple joy of going for a horseback ride with him.

Cord silently vowed to do much, much better in the future, whether Gracy was there or not. However, the thought of her leaving, of not looking across the kitchen table and seeing her head set aflame by the rays of sunshine that speared through the window, made him want to stand up and shout a declaration that she needed to be with them always.

Before he let the urge overtake him, Cord helped himself to a steak, cooked just the way he liked with pink in the center of the beef, and focused on eating his meal instead of ogling the beauty with her head bent over his son, helping him cut his meat.

When the meal was finished and Gracy stood at the sink washing dishes, Cord carried over dirty plates and stood behind her, hemming her in with his body. The soft fragrance of her ensnared his senses. He watched her movements as she wiped a rag over a plate and rinsed the suds away, appearing far more graceful than a woman with soap bubbles up to her wrists should look.

He pondered what her reaction would be if he took just one more step closer to her and pressed a kiss to the creamy skin exposed at the back of her neck. His fingers itched to brush aside the tendrils of hair that curled along her collar and trace along the column of her neck.

She'd likely spin around and break the plate over his head for even thinking such things if she had any idea of the direction of his wayward thoughts.

Humored by the picture in his head of the expression on her face, he swallowed back a chuckle, set the plate in the sink, then kissed her cheek.

Gracy turned her head ever so slightly, her look curious as she rinsed a glass and set it on a dish towel to dry. "You know, Cord, there's something I've been meaning to ask," she said in a whisper.

"What's that?" His voice was low and husky as he spoke. His hand settled on the curve of her waist as he leaned closer to her, enthralled not only by her scent, but also the slight blush blooming on her cheeks and the smile playing at the corners of her kissable lips.

"I want, Cord Granger, more than anything else this afternoon for you to take me up to the attic and …" She paused and turned so she faced him as he struggled to remember how to breathe with temptation only inches away.

"And?" he asked, unaware he spoke as he intently focused on those rosy lips of hers.

"And haul down the Christmas decorations. Bodie has been patiently waiting for days for you to do that. If you wait any longer, Christmas will be here and over."

Cord leaned back, not sure whether to laugh or rake a hand through his hair in exasperated frustration at the way she'd so easily enticed him. He should have known she was only teasing, which was evident by the mirth twinkling in her eyes and the humor on her lips.

Well, two could play that game.

He was sure she expected him to march straight up the stairs and haul down the decorations from the attic, which he'd meant to do multiple times. For some reason, he could hardly hold two thoughts together since Gracy had begun working for him.

"You know, Gracy," he said, sidling closer to her and bracing his hands against the sink, leaving her trapped in the circle of his arms. "Little girls who play with fire tend to get their fingers burned."

Only, when she looked up at him with yearning in her gaze, Cord felt like he was the one being consumed by flames. His head lowered toward hers and their lips had just barely brushed when Bodie ran into the room, full of giggles.

"What's this, Daddy? Is it a ball? Can I kick it like my other ball?"

Cord sighed and stepped back, grasping at the unraveled threads of his composure. Everything in him wanted to tell Bodie to kick the kissing ball until it was an obliterated pile of leaves, but he experienced the desire to kick it a few times himself, preferably at Luke.

Instead, he forced himself to smile and turned to face his son. "It's not a toy, Bode. Your cousin Maura made it as a decoration." He knelt beside Bodie, took the kissing ball from him, and dangled it from his index finger. "See, it hangs from this ribbon here. Where do you think we should put it?"

"I ... I ..." Bodie was so excited about the decoration, he raced out of the kitchen, scurried right back in, and grabbed Cord's hand. "Come on, Daddy. We gots to find a good place for it!"

Cord stood and let Bodie tug him from the room but not before glancing back at Gracy with a look of promise. Maybe next time he cornered her at the sink, he'd make sure the kissing ball was hanging overhead.

Chapter Fourteen

Gracy expelled a long breath that turned into a pillar of frosty tendrils curling toward the pearl gray sky in the frigid morning air. She rode Cider over to the barn at Juniper Creek Ranch and swung out of the saddle, grateful for the pair of woolen pants she wore beneath her skirts that kept her from freezing on the ride out from town.

"Morning, Miss Gracy," Tug said as he stepped out of the barn and hobbled toward her.

It had broken her heart to see the old cowboy walk with a limp after the injury to his knee, but at least he was still able to get around and continue working as the foreman of the ranch. She knew he didn't particularly enjoy the role of bunkhouse cook, but he'd told her it kept him busy, and it proved to the other hands he was willing to do whatever it took to keep things running smoothly at the ranch.

"Good morning, Tug. Do you think it's going to snow again today?" she asked, tipping back her head to look at the dark clouds moving closer.

"I'd bet my boots on it. In fact, I reckon it will start drifting down shortly. What'll you do if you get snowed in here?"

Gracy hadn't given the possibility a thought, but she shrugged as she loosened Cider's cinch and led the horse into the barn. "If that happens, Cord can sleep in the bunkhouse, and I'll stay in the house with Bodie."

Tug grinned. "You be sure to tell him I'll save the bunk by the door that catches the draft just for him."

Gracy smiled at her old friend and started to lift the saddle from Cider's back, but Tug nudged her out of the way and tipped his head toward the house. "Go on. I'll see to Cider. Bodie was chatting like a magpie at breakfast about all the Christmas decorations the two of you set out yesterday. He seemed particularly excited about some big ball."

Heat soaked into Gracy's cheeks as she recalled the kiss she'd almost shared with Cord in the kitchen yesterday. If it hadn't been for Bodie's timely arrival with the kissing ball, goodness only knows what might have happened. As it was, Cord had stammered to come up with an explanation of what the big ball with greens, silk flowers, and mistletoe tied with red ribbons represented.

Gracy made sure the kissing ball was hung in a spot she wasn't likely to get caught standing with Cord. If she'd found herself beneath that ball with him, there was no telling what either of them might do.

When Cord had returned from town yesterday looking so downhearted, she'd tried to tease him into a better mood. Calling him silly names and bantering harmless insults usually did the trick, but the sadness lingered in his eyes all through the meal.

The moment she'd realized he'd moved so close to her as she washed dishes, she'd wanted to lean back, to rest in his strength. Instead, she'd thought to coax him into bringing down the holiday decorations from the attic, only to find herself captive beneath the spell of his charm. When he'd gazed at her with his heart in his eyes, it had frightened her.

Gracy hadn't been kissed or held or even allowed a man close to her since Samuel. She longed for a simple touch of affection, the warmth of someone holding her hand or even just touching her in reassurance. Of course, her parents were affectionate, but it was far different to know a lover's touch.

She still hadn't decided if it was a good idea to pursue a relationship with Cord. What if people assumed she was only interested in him to get back her family's ranch? Or what if they gossiped that she'd behaved in an untoward manner staying at Juniper Creek Ranch all alone with him, even if it was during the day and not at night?

Do you really care what people think or say? a voice asked in her thoughts. Sometimes that voice sounded a lot like her brother Rob. He'd been the person Gracy went to for advice or help. Even though she'd been several years younger and he'd had his own family to think of, he'd always made time to listen to her and offer wisdom or direction. Most often, Rob had asked questions that had guided her to find her own solution, and she'd appreciated how much help he'd given her through the years.

Gracy sighed and gave Tug a tenuous smile, not wanting to cause him concern as she tumbled down the path of painful memories.

"I miss them too, Gracy." Tug squeezed her hand, as though he'd known where her thoughts had taken her. "It's a hard time of year to be without loved ones."

"It is, Tug, but I'm glad I'm here this year with you." Gracy gave him an impetuous hug, lifted her skirts, and ran to the house and up the back steps. The dogs woofed and wiggled as they jumped up from their bed by the door, eager for attention. After petting them both, she tapped once on the door, then stepped inside.

"I'm clean enough, Daddy!" she heard Bodie shouting and the sound of water splashing.

"I don't know how you possibly got that dirty that fast," Cord said, sounding like he was at the end of his patience.

Gracy removed her scarf, mittens, coat, and boots, hastily hanging them by the door, then hurried down the hallway to the bathroom.

"What's going on?" she asked as she stepped into the room to see Bodie in the tub, covered in streaks of black, while Cord knelt beside it, shirtless, with a washcloth in one hand and a bar of soap in the other.

His expression held relief as he glanced up at her. "I didn't hear you come in. Bodie spilled a bottle of ink all over himself."

"Oh, that explains the black," she said, rolling up the sleeves of her dress and trying not to notice the muscles that rippled and bulged on Cord's chest and arms. The sight of his form and the way he looked at her with a mixture of humor over Bodie's mishaps and something that seemed a lot like desire made her wish she'd taken a moment to pull off the heavy woolen pants she still wore. "Perhaps I should give it a try. We can't have one of the sheep for the Christmas program with a black-smeared face, can we?"

"I been practicing to be a sheep, Gracy. Listen to me," Bodie said, spinning in the tub, sending water sloshing over the sides. "Listen, I'm a sheep! *Baa! Baa! Baa!*"

"That's very good, Bodie. Now you sit still, and let's see if we can't get you cleaned up." Gracy held her hands out to Cord, taking the washcloth and soap from him. "Do you have any alcohol?"

He gave her the rag and soap, then stood. He smirked, making the lines around his eyes and mouth deepen in a way she found completely alluring and unnerving, given his current state of undress. "A little early in the day for booze, isn't it, Gracy?"

She scowled and swatted him with the wet cloth. "You numbskull, it isn't for me. I want to see if it will take off the ink."

Cord didn't look the least bit chagrined as he leaned toward her and kissed her cheek. "I'm just funning you. I've got some whiskey for medicinal purposes.

"Then please retrieve it, and put a shirt on, for heaven's sake!"

Cord stood there, chest bare, and had the audacity to wink at her as he tightened his muscles, making his form take on an even more impressive appearance.

Gracy felt the heat burning not only in her cheeks but also up her neck and over her ears until her entire head felt like it might be aflame. She spun around, dropped to her knees, and began scrubbing Bodie.

"What on earth were you doing to spill ink all over you?" she asked the little boy who closed one eye and scrunched up his nose as she attacked his chin with the soapy cloth.

"I was just playing with Mup, and pretending he could fly. But I bumped Daddy's ink and it went blop all over me and Mup." His lip rolled out in a pout. "Do you think Mup will be mad?"

Gracy smiled at him as she soaped the rag again and gently rubbed at a blob of ink on his ear lobe. "I don't think Mup will care, sweetheart, but you'll have to be more careful when you play around your father's desk."

Bodie sighed. "I know. I'm sorry." He looked like he was about to cry as his lip began to quiver.

"Daddy told me I have to clean up my messes so it doesn't make more work for you."

Gracy thought about giving Cord an earful about making his son feel guilty for making extra work for her when he often trekked manure and mud inside on her clean floors. She knew he didn't do it intentionally, nor was he even aware of it, but she felt like she spent an hour a day mopping up after him. If she were married to Cord, she'd set him straight about walking into the house while wearing dirty boots.

An image of Cord as he stood there winking at her with all that glorious skin on display made her blush all over again.

"Do I even want to know what you're thinking?" Cord asked as he held a full bottle of whiskey out toward her. She took some satisfaction in seeing it hadn't been opened and had a coating of dust on the neck, indicating it had been sitting somewhere for a while. At least she wouldn't have to worry about Cord being someone who imbibed frequently.

She just needed to concern herself with her undeniable attraction to the handsome man who had put on a shirt but had failed to take time to button it. The way the plaid flannel flapped with each movement he made offered her far too clear a vision of that broad chest with a mat of soft brown hair across it.

Forcing her thoughts away from Cord's raw masculinity to removing the ink on Bodie, Gracy poured whiskey onto the washcloth and scrubbed Bodie's hand. She didn't know if it was the warm water, the many applications of soap and scrubbing, or the alcohol, but the ink finally came off. The only spot she couldn't get out was a splatter above his right eye, and that was only because he hollered every time she tried to get close to it like he thought she was going to poke out his eyeball.

By the time she finished, Bodie's little fingers were as wrinkled as prunes, but he was clean.

"Come on, let's get you dried off and dressed," Gracy said, holding a thick towel for him as he climbed out of the tub. She briskly rubbed the towel over his arms and back, then told him to go to the kitchen while she got him a change of clothes. It would be warmer for him to dress there than anywhere else in the house, even though the furnace kept the rooms comfortable.

Gracy hurried upstairs and retrieved clothes for Bodie, then returned to the kitchen. Bodie sat at the table, grinning and humming. Cord had just dunked half a cookie into a glass of milk sitting in front of the little boy.

Before she could object, they each crammed bites of cookie into their mouths and grinned.

Gracy knew Cord thought Bodie looked just like his deceased wife, but she could see so many similar mannerisms between father and son. Even the cowlick that always stuck out on Bodie's head was similar to one Cord tried to comb into submission. Bodie might have his mother's dark hair and eyes, but his smile, his nose, the shape of his chin, and even his ears were all from Cord.

The fact that Gracy had spent enough time studying the man to know that left her disturbed.

She needed to fasten her focus on her job and nothing more. Cord might tease and flirt, but Gracy had the idea he was a long way from ready to think about opening his heart again.

"I'll go clean up the ink," she said, handing Cord the clothes she'd brought down for Bodie.

"I think I got most of it, but see what you think," he said, lifting an ink-stained hand and motioning toward the door.

Gracy went to the room Cord used as an office and eyed the floor around the desk. A few ink splatters remained, so she got down on her hands and knees to see to the task of scrubbing them away. The mindless action of cleaning gave her the time she needed to tug her thoughts together.

She heard the patter of Bodie's feet and a longer, heavier stride before she glanced up and saw the two Granger males standing in the doorway.

"I'm sorry I made extra work for you, Gracy. I'll try not to spill again." Bodie looked repentant, with his lip rolled out in a pout and his eyes wide and damp with unshed tears.

"It's okay, sweetheart. Accidents happen." She sat back on her heels and held out her arms to him.

Bodie raced across the room, launching himself against her. Gracy smiled, breathing in his clean scent, loving the feel of his affectionate little hug as his arms squeezed her neck, then he kissed her cheek.

"Love you, Gracy."

"I love you, too, Bodie." She released him and rose to her feet, wiping her hands on the rag she still held. "There isn't much we can do about Mup, but I think he looks quite dashing as a pinto."

She handed the toy horse to Bodie. Although she'd tried to remove the two big splotches of black ink, it had soaked into the wood of the toy.

Bodie cocked his head and looked from Mup to her. "What's pinto?"

"It's the color of a horse. It means it has white splotches with another color. Just like Mup has now."

Bodie held the toy up and ran over to where Cord lounged, now fully dressed, against the door. "I gots a pinto, Daddy. Mup is a pinto!"

"He sure is, son." Cord ruffled the boy's hair, but his eyes lingered on Gracy, making her nervously shove pins back into her hair that had loosened as she'd cleaned first Bodie and then the floor.

"I should um …" Gracy had no idea what she was going to say, or what she'd planned to do. Something in Cord's gaze left her so flustered, she couldn't keep track of her thoughts. Thankfully, Bodie was there to serve as a buffer to whatever it was that sparked between her and Cord.

Neither of them could deny something arced between them no matter how much they might want to. Fight it? Yes. But claim there was nothing pulling them together? That would be an outright lie.

And Gracy never lied. She didn't think Cord would either, even if the two of them did their best to ignore the attraction hanging between them like a heavy weight that pulled them toward one another.

"I'd better get to work," Cord said, shoving away from the doorframe and taking a step back into the hall. "If I didn't mention it yesterday, the decorations look nice, Gracy. Thank you for putting them up and allowing Bodie to help. He loved every minute of it."

"I had fun with him too. You're welcome, Cord." Gracy twisted the rag she'd been using to scrub the floor between her hands, nervous and dry-mouthed as Cord held her gaze instead of leaving.

For a fleeting, insane moment, she wondered what he'd do if she crossed the room and kissed him like she so often dreamed of doing. It wasn't just that he was a handsome man by anyone's standards. Her interest in him went far deeper than the surface. He was so good with Bodie, so patient with him, and gentle. Tug sang his praises, which spoke volumes to her because the foreman generally erred on the side of critical. Her parents thought he was wonderful, and so many of Gracy's friends had commented about his being a good, kind man.

Gracy admired him for starting over after losing his wife and trying to build a new life for himself and Bodie. It couldn't be easy moving away from the only home he'd ever known or attempting to raise an active, lively boy like Bodie on his own, but from what she could see, Cord was a loving, caring father and an honorable, trustworthy man, and he'd been a good friend to her in the weeks since she'd been back in Hardman.

The future was uncertain. Gracy might yet have to pack her bags and seek employment elsewhere, but for now—for today—she was content to be at

Juniper Creek Ranch with a little boy who loved her and a man who made her remember she was a desirable woman.

"I'd better get going," Cord said, pointing behind him toward the door.

"I'll have lunch ready an hour early today. Bodie needs to be at the church by one for the Christmas program practice. If you don't object, I thought we could ride together into town on Cider."

Cord smirked at her. "You think all three of us will fit on Cider? She's a fine mare, but it might be more of a load than she wants to carry."

Gracy tossed the rag at him, and he caught it with a chuckle. "That's fine, Gracy. If you want me to hitch up the sleigh and take you, I will."

"No. Bodie and I will both enjoy the ride. If you want to come to town later to pick him up, you could join Mama and Papa and me for supper."

"That sounds like a fine plan." Cord backed up a few steps, then tossed the rag back to her. "Do you still want to go with us tomorrow morning to get a Christmas tree?"

"I'd love to, but if you'd prefer, I can stay with Bodie. It will be too cold for him to be out traipsing in the woods."

"No. Tug will keep an eye on him. I'd like you to go with us. I'll see you in a bit." With that, he turned and left. A blast of cold air and the sound of the door clicking shut marked his departure.

Gracy returned to scrubbing the rest of the ink off the floor and encouraged Bodie to stay with her, having him recite the alphabet, review colors, and count as high as he could go.

She cooked thick ham steaks for lunch and served them with hot biscuits, fried potatoes flavored with chopped onion, and sliced fresh pears from a large basket of fruit Cord had purchased and stored in the cellar. Dessert was rice pudding dotted with raisins. Cord seemed to be partial to puddings and custards, which were, in Gracy's opinion, one of the easiest things to make. While Cord cleaned up his second serving of the pudding, Gracy hurried to do the dishes.

"Bodie, we're going into town for the church program practice. I'll be ready to go in fifteen minutes, so when the hands on the clock are here and here," Gracy showed him where the hands on the clock would be, "we'll ride Cider to Hardman. I need you to go wash your hands and face and visit the necessary."

"I can help him," Cord started to rise, but Bodie hopped out of his chair and raced from the room.

"He likes to be independent," Gracy said, smiling after Bodie and then turning back to the dishes. She wondered if Cord would once again try to hem her in and steal a kiss. Although, was it stealing if she was more than willing to give it to him? She thought probably not, but decided kissing him needed to be the last thing on her mind or she'd never be able to focus on getting Bodie to town. Pastor Dodd had asked if she could stay for the practice to help Brynn and Percy as they attempted to get all the children to do what they were supposed to.

"I'm sure he didn't get that from me," Cord said, shoveling in the last bite of the pudding, then carrying his bowl over to her. When he slid it into the soapy water in the sink, his fingers connected with hers. His thumb caressed the back of her hand in slow circles until Gracy felt so languid, it was a wonder she didn't pool into a heap on the floor.

She turned to lambast Cord, but when she moved her head, she found him so near, she could see both green and blue flecks in his eyes that had suddenly darkened.

"Daddy! I need helps!" Bodie called from down the hall, and Cord blew out a breath that warmed the skin of Gracy's neck.

She stood stiff and tense until he pulled his hand from the dishwater, dabbed his fingers on a towel, then strode from the room in long strides.

Gracy hastened to finish the dishes, dry them, and put them away. She removed the apron she wore and retreated to the bathroom, where she smoothed her hair, wiped flour off her cheek, and pulled on the wool pants she'd slipped off earlier.

After checking to make sure she looked presentable, she went to the back door, tugged on her boots, and checked to make sure she had her warm mittens.

The sound of Bodie's footsteps thudding down the stairs preceded his presence in the hall. "Daddy made me wear two pairs of socks, Gracy. He said he doesn't want my toes to freeze and fall off!" Bodie leaned against her and lifted a foot as she held out one of his boots.

"No, we don't what those cute little toes to turn into ice chunks." Gracy eased his foot into his boot, pulling it on, then repeating the process with the

SHANNA HATFIELD

other. She made sure Bodie had on a heavy sweater before she helped him with his coat. She buttoned it up, wrapped a scarf around his neck, tugged on his stocking cap, and held his mittens while he stuffed his hands inside them.

Gracy wrapped a scarf around her ears and neck, slipped on her mittens, then motioned for Bodie to precede her outside. They walked down the porch steps and around the house to find Cord standing there with Cider saddled and ready to go.

"Thank you for doing that," Gracy said, taking the reins from him and swinging onto the back of her horse before Cord could offer his assistance. His eyebrows shot upward, and she didn't know if he'd caught a glimpse of her britches, or if he was surprised she could agilely mount the horse.

Cord picked up Bodie and set him in the saddle in front of her. "Shall I meet you at your folks' house?"

"Yes. After the practice, Bodie and I are going to the community hall. It's where several of the women decided to gather to do final fittings for the program costumes. We would have done it at the church, but the choir requested extra time to practice, and a crew is in the basement touching up the props for the program. Without anywhere else to fit the costumes, Alex Guthry arranged for us to meet at the community hall. Lila and Filly are providing the refreshments. We'll likely be there an hour or so before we go to Mama and Papa's house."

"That's fine, Gracy. I'll catch up with you at your folks' house. If you want, I'd be happy to take everyone out for supper so you and your mother don't have to cook."

"I'll mention that to her. She's planning to drop by to watch the practice." Gracy clucked her tongue, and Cider started down the lane.

"Bye, Daddy!" Bodie waved excitedly as he leaned over Gracy's arm. "Bye!"

"Mind your manners, Bode, and have fun!" Cord called after them.

Gracy fought the urge to turn around and look at Cord one more time, but she kept her focus forward and answered Bodie's multitude of questions as they rode into town. He wanted to know the names of every bird they saw, why snow was white and Christmas trees were green, and when it would be warm outside again.

By the time they reached the church, she was exhausted, both from answering his questions and keeping him from slipping out of the saddle as he constantly leaned over or stretched or turned to look at something. Bodie had a quick mind that kept her on her toes, but she loved seeing his face light up when he learned something new.

"Do you remember your part in the program, Bodie?" she asked as she picked him up and set him onto the walk someone had shoveled in front of the church.

"Yep. When Percy gives me the signal, I say *baa* three times."

"That's right!" Gracy said, giving him a pleased smile as she swung off the horse and looped the reins around one of the hitching posts.

"Gracy!" her mother called from across the street. Bodie would have run to her, but Gracy grabbed his hand and kept him from darting in front of a passing wagon.

"Grammy!" Bodie called, waving a hand over his head. "Hi, Grammy!"

"Hi, honey," Cleo said as she rushed across the street and swept the little boy into a hug. "Oh, it's good to see you, Bodie. It's been ages since I've had a hug."

Bodie wrapped his arms around her neck and kissed her cheek with a noisy smack. "I missed you, Grammy."

"And I missed you, sweet boy. Are you ready for your practice?"

"Yep! I gets to say *baa, baa, baa*."

"Yes, you do." Cleo settled her arm around Gracy's waist and gave it a squeeze as the three of them walked into the church.

"Before I forget, Mama, Cord is going to come pick up Bodie later and offered to take us out to dinner. What do you think? Would you enjoy an evening of not cooking?"

Cleo nodded. "I'd love that. We'll plan on it. I do have sweet rolls rising that I need to bake this afternoon. I can take Cider back to the house when I leave so you don't have to worry about the horse later. You are still planning to go work on costumes after the practice, aren't you?"

"Yes. That's the plan. Filly and Lila were going to bring refreshments, and I think a few of the older girls will keep the younger children entertained. The choir requested extra time to practice this afternoon, otherwise, we'd just stay here."

"It's nice the community hall is available now. It's a great thing Gray and Claire Carter decided to turn that old packing shed into something useful, even if it is across the street from that deplorable saloon."

"The location isn't the best, but there haven't really been any issues that have arisen from the Red Lantern."

"We'd better hush, or we'll be in trouble for uttering that name in the church." Cleo grinned at Gracy as they removed their coats and helped Bodie with his before he raced to join his cousin Patrick and the other children as they gathered at the front of the church.

Dora Granger played the piano for the play, and both Cleo and Gracy helped keep the children somewhat quiet until it was their turn to perform.

The practice went smoothly, and Percy reminded all the children to follow them to the community hall, where they would try on their costumes.

In a flurry of mittens and coats, everyone was soon racing across the street and down the side alley to the community hall, where they gathered in a smaller room. A cheery fire in the fireplace provided a warm welcome in the room. Filly and Lila had set out platters of cookies as well as cups of hot cider and hot chocolate.

It didn't take long to make sure each child had a costume, although several of them required alterations.

Cleo took two angel costumes with her and went home to bake her sweet rolls.

Bodie begged and pleaded to spend time with Patrick. At Filly's agreement, Gracy let him accompany them home. She remained behind with Junie Grove, Alex Guthry, and Abby Dodd to make the necessary alterations to the costumes. Once they finished, Pastor Dodd and Percy would move them all to the church and have them ready for the program tomorrow evening.

Gracy poured a second cup of cider, helped herself to a soft sour cream cookie, and went back to lengthening the hem on a robe for one of the wise men.

In all the years she'd participated in the play, she'd never given a thought to how much work went into the set and costumes, or how many parents and community members were involved in the production.

"Tell us how you like working for Mr. Granger," Junie said, bumping Gracy's elbow and grinning. "He's a handsome one. Looks a lot like Luke did at that age."

She shrugged and concentrated on making even stitches. Sewing was not something she loved to do, but her mother had made sure she was proficient at it. "I like working for him well enough. I love being back out at the ranch, and Bodie is wonderful. Yesterday, he asked me if enough soap bubbles were piled together if they would carry him up to heaven so he could say hi to his mother."

"Oh, my gracious." Junie pulled a handkerchief from her sleeve and dabbed at her nose. "The things youngsters say just can touch your soul sometimes."

"That's so true. And other times, they make you want to rip out your hair." Abby grinned as her fingers flew, stitching a sleeve into the costume the boy playing Joseph would wear. "Erin gets so mopey missing Toby Guthry that she nearly wears out my patience."

Alex gave her a commiserating nod. "Tia and Adam said Toby is equally as annoying and pathetic when it comes to missing Erin. Who would have thought their childhood infatuation with each other would grow so strong and remain so true all these years?"

"They do seem quite taken with each other," Junie observed, then she gave Gracy a sly glance. "Speaking of being taken with someone, I saw Cord watching you after church on Sunday. Why, the man could hardly take his eyes off you."

Gracy blushed and shook her head. "I probably had something on my face, or my collar was askew."

Abby laughed. "I don't think so, Gracy. Cord seems quite infatuated with you. He never looked at anyone else the way he looks at you, at least not that we've seen."

Alex grinned at Gracy. "You might as well surrender to the inevitable. It's easier that way."

Gracy looked at Alex. The woman had taught school for many years in Hardman and occasionally performed a magic show since she'd worked as a prestidigitator before she'd married Arlan. "What do you mean the inevitable?"

Alex offered her a knowing smile. "You're in love with Cord. It's as plain as the nose on your face. He's in love with you. It's only a matter of time before you both figure things out and embark on your happily ever after."

"I don't—" Gracy stopped mid-sentence. "Does something smell like smoke?"

The other women sniffed the air and stood as a loud popping sound echoed through the building, followed by a boom that rattled the high windows. Smoke began pouring into the room from the door that opened into the alley.

Alex tried to open the door, but it wouldn't budge. She and Gracy both pushed against it, but found it impossible to move.

"Let's go out the front door," Abby said, grabbing an armful of costumes and rushing from the room.

The entire building rapidly filled with smoke, and through the windows, the women could see flames blazing outside.

The front door was locked, and Alex, who'd been given the keys from Claire Carter, fumbled to find the one that would open it.

"If you aren't already, now would be a good time to pray," Alex said, glancing over her shoulder, then coughing.

The acrid odor in the air burned Gracy's eyes and stung her lungs as she, like the others, struggled to breathe.

If they didn't get out soon, Gracy hated to think what would happen.

Chapter Fifteen

Zeke Daniels hated winter. Hated his life. Hated that he'd lost the card game he'd spent hours playing even though he was sure he had a winning hand. What little money he had left, he'd spent on enough whiskey to make him forget the reasons it hurt too much to remember his past.

When he didn't have a dime left, the barkeep tossed him out and told him not to come back until he could afford it.

"Too cold. Too hungry," Zeke muttered, stumbling around the Red Lantern into the alley. An old wagon sat behind the business with the back full of whiskey barrels.

Zeke glanced around to make sure no one was watching, then shuffled his way through the snow to the wagon, hoping the barrels would be full. He grabbed one and tipped it toward him. Just his luck, they were all empty.

With a glance down the alley at the stone doorstep someone had cleared of snow, then back at the wagon, Zeke stumbled to the back of the wagon and pushed with all his might. It creaked and rolled forward a few inches. He repeated the process until the wagon stood over those stones, then he took a book of matches from his pocket, yanked a sign off the door the wagon now sat in front of, and proceeded to build a fire with the paper and pieces of a broken barrel.

"Much better," he mumbled as he sat beneath the wagon on the stone step, assured the snow that would likely soon begin to fall wouldn't reach him beneath the wagon.

The wood burned fast and hot, and he held his hands out to it, grateful for the warmth. He needed more wood, so he took one of the big barrels from the wagon and kicked at it until it began to break apart. He dumped the pieces on the fire, watching the flames lick greedily at the whiskey-soaked wood.

Zeke scooted back beneath the wagon. One minute, he was enjoying the toasty warmth, and the next something above him exploded. He scrambled to his feet and backed up a few steps, watching as the wagon caught fire. Another boom, one so loud it made Zeke's ears ring, rocked the wagon, and it listed to one side, falling against the door he'd just been sitting in front of.

Despite the snow on the ground, the fire quickly spread, catching the community hall on fire and somehow, the Red Lantern Saloon as well.

Stunned by the flames, and by what he'd done, Zeke stood rooted to the spot until another barrel exploded, causing the windows in the high wall of the community hall to burst and rain down lethal shards of glass.

Zeke raised his arms above his head, feeling glass slice into his skin. Then he heard the screams coming from inside the community hall and the saloon. On unsteady feet, Zeke banged on the back door of the saloon, but no one opened it. Without any idea what to do, Zeke hustled around to the front door of the community hall. The door was locked, but he tried to shoulder it open.

The last thing he remembered was ramming into it over and over again before pain pierced his back and his left arm. Then the world turned dark, and Zeke slumped to the ground.

Chapter Sixteen

Luke's words about giving Gracy jewelry as a bonus continued to taunt Cord all afternoon. He cleaned up and headed into town an hour earlier than he'd planned so he could stop by Bruner's Mercantile and see what options they had. If he didn't find anything there he liked, he could always visit the jewelry shop, but he wasn't all that fond of the owner.

Cord debated all the way into town about what he would purchase for Gracy. Gifts of jewelry were considered inappropriate for a man to give a woman who was not a relative, but Cord thought perhaps an exception could be made regarding Gracy. Bodie was convinced Cleo and Everett were his grandparents, and his son now adored Gracy, despite their rocky first meeting. As for Cord, he thought of Gracy as … well, he wasn't sure, but he thought of her often. Thought well of her. Thought of the feisty woman in terms of someone he'd like to spend a long time getting to know.

Besides, no one needed to know, other than Gracy, that the gift was from him. Maybe he could give it to her from Bodie? Cord quickly discarded that thought, mindful of Bodie's tendency to say whatever popped into his head. Goodness only knew who all Bodie would tell.

No. Cord would purchase something special for a special friend and that was that.

He stopped the sleigh outside Bruner's store, waved at his cousin Lila as she paused with her two little ones before going inside the newspaper office down the street, and glanced up at the snow-laden clouds moving across the sky. Cord figured it would be a cold, snowy ride home. At least he'd remembered to toss in a few extra blankets to keep Bodie warm on the way home.

Cord hopped out of the sleigh and entered the store, hoping Bodie had fun at the Christmas program practice and trying on his sheep costume. A vision of his son down on all fours, making a baaing sound and smiling with his cowlick sticking up made him grin as he tipped his head to Aleta Bruner.

She was busy with a customer, but when she finished, she walked over to him with a friendly greeting.

"Welcome to the store, Cord. How may I assist you today?"

Cord glanced at her from where he hovered above a large case full of jewelry. It included everything from the cheapest golden bands to expensive gold watches.

"I'm just looking for a little something," he said, studying the brooches. A white gold oval with a bright ruby caught his eye, but he also liked a long bar design that had a sapphire in the center. His gaze landed on a silver brooch with a filigree pattern. Small diamonds encircled a gorgeous emerald in the center. Cord had noticed Gracy tended to favor that particular hue of green. He could envision the fine piece of jewelry fastened to her coat or any number of her dresses.

"That one," he said, pointing to the emerald brooch. "Can you wrap it for me, Aleta?"

"Certainly." She lifted the brooch from the case and handed it to him to examine as she retrieved a black jewelry box lined with emerald velvet. "You might want to see this. It matches the brooch." She set out a ring with a large diamond surrounded by emeralds with a design that exactly matched the brooch. It wasn't any trifling piece of jewelry but something meant to last a lifetime.

Without giving himself time to mull it over, Cord nodded. "I'll take them both, but please wrap them separately."

Aleta practically beamed at him. "You made a perfect choice for her, Cord. She'll love these."

Although Cord chose not to acknowledge of whom she spoke, they both knew the pieces were intended for Gracy.

Cord added a few more gifts for friends to his purchases, paid Aleta, and promised to return in a while to pick them up after she had a chance to wrap them.

He left the store and was on his way to Luke's to check on Bodie's Christmas present when he heard what sounded like an explosion. He'd just stepped in front of the bakery, and the windows rattled from the force of the explosion. Black smoke billowed into the sky.

"Fire!" he heard someone shout, and took off running toward the building the volunteer fire department used to house their equipment. Cord got there just as Luke was unlocking the door.

"What happened?" Cord asked as he ran inside and whipped off his coat, tugging on one of the heavy canvas coats the volunteers used.

"I don't know, but I received a telephone call from the Red Lantern Saloon saying there was a fire in the alley behind them and it was spreading fast." Luke started the auto they used for fire calls then yanked off his suit coat and hat, tugged on a fire coat, and hopped into the vehicle.

Cord jumped in, and they drove out of the building, heading toward the thickening smoke. They'd just turned off the main street by the Red Lantern Saloon, when flames shot out windows and from the roof, indicating the building was too far gone to save.

Cord's heart sank to his feet and he felt like he might be physically ill when he realized it wasn't the only building about to burn to the ground. The community hall, where Bodie and Gracy were working on Christmas program costumes, was engulfed in flames. Windows popped and crackled, timbers creaked, and the sound of the fire was a loud roar.

Unable to bear the thought of his son or the woman he loved being trapped inside that inferno, Cord leaped out of the moving vehicle. He raced to where the front door should have been, but the upper story had collapsed over it. Heat unlike anything he'd ever experienced sucked the breath right out of him. His skin felt like it might blister just standing there, but he had to get inside. He had to!

Cord took a step forward, but a firm hand gripped his arm and pulled him back.

"Let me go, Luke!" he shouted to be heard above the fire and the screams of people escaping the boarding house on the other side of the community hall. "I have to save Bodie and Gracy!"

"They're safe, Cord. They're safe. Bodie's at home with Filly. Gracy is right there." Luke turned him toward the church. Cord looked across the street to see a soot-covered Gracy, her hair tumbling around her face, coughing into a handkerchief as she and Alex Guthry leaned against each other where they sat on the church steps. Around them, costumes for the church program littered the ground like they'd floated out of the sky with the ashes that turned the snow gray.

Cord didn't stop. Didn't think. He ran across the street, dropped to his knees in front of Gracy, and pulled her into a tight hug.

"I thought I'd lost you, Gracy. I thought I'd lost you," he repeated over and over, giving thanks that she was unharmed. Until the moment he thought he might lose her, he hadn't fully realized how much he needed her or how deeply he loved her.

Gracy melted against him, her arms wrapping around him as she buried her face against his coat. The sharp, acrid odor of smoke clung to her hair, and he could see places where her clothes and hair had been singed, but none of that mattered. Gracy was alive and well, and Bodie was safe at Granger House.

Cord felt like he'd been given a huge gift wrapped in a blessing to know they both were safe.

Never again would he take his time with either of them for granted. Life was too short and far too precious to keep putting off for tomorrow what they should treasure today. Cord should have learned that lesson when he'd lost Helen, but somehow her death had made him even more resistant to embracing life and all the joys and sorrows it might bring.

Until he'd met Gracy, he'd just been going through the motions of living, lingering in the dark shadows of his memories. It wasn't until he'd walked into his barn and seen her and experienced her fiery personality, that his world had suddenly flooded with color, like a rainbow bursting through the clouds. Gracy had taught him to laugh again, to find joy in each day, and to love.

"Cord," she said, although her voice was muffled as he held one hand buried in the hair at the back of her head, keeping her close to his chest. "Cord," she said again, pushing against him. "You're going to smother me."

"Oh. I'm sorry, Gracy. I'm so sorry."

She leaned back and smiled at him. He could see the humor in her gaze along with relief. "I'm fine, Cord. I'm truly fine, and Bodie is safe at Granger House."

"I was so scared you were in that building, Gracy. If you had been, if anything had happened to you, I don't know what I would have done." Cord had so much he wanted to say to her, so many things he wanted to discuss, but now wasn't the time. Not with most of the town gathering around them to watch the fire destroy the Red Lantern Saloon, the community hall, the boarding house, and two small homes.

Cord glanced over his shoulder to see other volunteer firefighters arriving and knew he needed to go help them try to contain the fire before it burned down half the town. "I have to go, Gracy, but I'll come see you later."

"Be careful," Gracy said, giving him a tight hug before she let him go and leaned back. "I'll be waiting for you."

"I'll count on that." Cord didn't care who was watching as he leaned forward and brushed a light kiss over her lips. He turned and jogged across the street, joining Luke, Blake, Tom Grove, Gray Carter, and several others as they attempted to subdue the fire.

Hours later, darkness had fallen and the temperatures had dropped. Snow had begun to fall in earnest about the time the sun had set, which had helped with the fire. Still, the volunteer firefighters felt compelled to stay and keep watch to make certain no other buildings were destroyed.

Cord felt almost sorry for the drunk who'd accidentally started the blaze when he'd been trying to get warm. He'd heard from Abby Dodd who'd brought hot coffee and sandwiches to them that the man had been trying to break down the door so she, Junie, Alex, and Gracy could get out. A timber had fallen on him and knocked him out, and he'd suffered burns on his arm and back. Right now, he was at the doctor's office, and the owner of the Red Lantern Saloon had made threats to have him sent to prison for the rest of his miserable life.

Cord sent up a prayer for the man because he was certain one day the damage he'd done would come back to haunt him. He also prayed with gratitude that no lives had been lost that day. Buildings could be rebuilt, injuries could be treated, but a life lost … Cord just couldn't bear the thought since it could easily have been Gracy or one of the other women he admired and considered among his friends.

Weary, filthy, cold, wet, and hungry, Cord let Luke talk him into staying the night at his house instead of traveling back to the ranch.

Although he'd been desperate to go see Gracy, it was far too late when he and Luke finally returned the auto to the volunteer fire station and walked through the snowy night to Granger House.

Tomorrow would be soon enough to tell Gracy how much she meant to him. Christmas Eve was a time of miracles and magic. He hoped that meant she'd return his love.

Chapter Seventeen

"Oh, Mama!" Gracy clasped her hands beneath her chin and grinned at her mother. "You look amazing."

Cleo spun in a slow circle, then giggled like a schoolgirl. She'd pinned her white hair in an exaggerated pouf on top of her head with dozens of tiny curls framing her face. She wore a red velvet gown with a wide sweeping skirt, all trimmed in a two-inch band of white fur. Gracy had purchased a little pot of rouge from the mercantile and added color to her mother's cheeks.

With a pair of spectacles perched on her nose, her mother looked exactly as Gracy had always envisioned Mrs. Claus might appear.

"You definitely look like Saint Nick's wife." Gracy kissed her mother's cheek, then laughed as Cleo twirled around a second time, sending the skirt belling around her.

"Ho! Ho! Ho! Who is this gorgeous Christmas fairy?" Everett boomed as he sauntered into the room wearing a red velvet jacket with pants that he'd tucked into a pair of tall black boots. He'd had to add padding at his waist in the form of a pillow held in place by a wide black leather belt, but with the white beard he'd allowed to grow out and a twinkle in his eye, he made a convincing Santa Claus.

Dora Granger Rutherford had asked if Everett and Cleo would be willing to play Santa and Mrs. Claus at the annual Christmas Eve Carnival this year. Despite yesterday's tragic fire, everyone had agreed a celebration was what the town needed.

Dora and her husband Merle had even opened their home to the two families who'd lost their houses in the fire. Several members of the community had taken in those who'd been staying at the boarding house until other arrangements could be made. Thankfully, since the fire had started in the afternoon and several boarders had already left for the holidays, there weren't many people there when the flames had jumped from the community hall to the roof of the boarding house.

Sadly, the community hall had burned to the ground. All that remained were the fireplaces and a few charred timbers. The Red Lantern Saloon was also a total loss. Once the fire had reached the interior, with all the liquor that was stored there, the fire had exploded, and the building had burned in a matter of minutes. One of the saloon girls who had been asleep had been burned on both legs as she'd escaped, but other than that, injuries had remained at a minimum.

For several long minutes that felt like they stretched for half an eternity, Gracy had wondered if she and the other women would perish in the building when none of them could find the key to unlock the front door. They'd heard banging on it and responded with screams for help, but Gracy had been the one to say a prayer and jam a key they'd already tried three times into the lock. It had clicked and they'd barreled outside, arms loaded with costumes, to find a stranger passed out on the front walk. It appeared he'd been knocked unconscious by a falling timber, and he had burns on his back and arm, but from what Gracy had heard, the doctor thought he'd eventually recover.

The gossip was that the man had been drunk and started the fire by using whiskey barrels as firewood in the alley between the saloon and the community hall. When the flames had hit the barrels soaked in whiskey, they'd started to explode. The wagon the drunk had been sitting under to get out of the weather had landed against the back door of the community hall room Gracy and her friends had been in, preventing their escape. It was probably a good thing they hadn't been able to open the door because it would have sucked the fire straight into the community hall before they could safely exit.

In those moments when she, Abby, Alex, and Junie had been frantic to get the door unlocked, Gracy had thought of her loved ones. Of never seeing her parents, or Bodie, or especially Cord again. She'd realized then how much she loved Cord Granger and wanted to be a part of his life every day. Not as his housekeeper or cook. Not just as a friend. She wanted to be his wife and spend however much time God granted them on earth together.

When he'd run over to her as she and Alex had sat on the porch steps, trying to drag fresh air into their smoke-filled lungs, she'd seen the panic and fear on his face. He'd been nearly beside himself as he'd held her tight and repeatedly told her he thought he'd lost her.

She knew they needed to talk, to share their feelings, but he'd had responsibilities to help with the fire.

Gracy had gone home to bathe and rest, hoping Cord would stop by later, but her father had gone to check on the fire and had come back to report the volunteer crew was keeping an eye on it even though it was late. She'd heard from Filly that morning that it had been well past midnight when Cord and Luke had finally made it home.

Although she had no idea what the day would bring, she knew at some point she and Cord would have a chance to connect and talk. At least she hoped they would.

For now, she needed to escort Santa and Mrs. Claus to the Christmas Eve celebration being held at Dora and Merle's mansion. Everyone brought something to share, and the Grangers filled in the gaps with roasted beef, gallons of mashed potatoes, and more pies than anyone thought could be eaten in a month, yet there were rarely leftovers.

Gracy looked at her parents, uncertain who was more excited: her mother or her father. They both were nearly as giddy as the children they were sure to please with their portrayal of Father Christmas and his bride.

"Come on, ol' Santie Claus," Gracy said with an exaggerated western twang, grinning as she tugged on her father's hand. "It's time for you two to make your grand entry."

"Let me get my coat," Cleo said, lifting her best black wool coat from a hook by the door and sliding her arms in the sleeves as Everett held it for her.

Gracy slipped on a green coat that matched the green velvet skirt she wore with a green and red plaid shirtwaist. The last time she'd worn the outfit, she'd caught Cord's eyes on her several times, as though he couldn't help but look at her. She hoped that meant he liked the outfit—and her.

"Ready, beautiful ladies?" Everett asked as he picked up one of the baskets Gracy and her mother had packed with food. Gracy picked up a smaller basket and handed it to her mother, then hefted the last one.

Her father held the door as she and her mother trooped outside. Three abreast, they strolled down the walk, making their way to Dora and Merle's home.

"I just now noticed that lovely sprig of holly in your hair, Gracy. It's the perfect festive touch."

Cleo smiled at her as they waited for a wagon and a sleigh to pass by when they reached the corner. Friends waved and shouted holiday wishes as they headed toward the party.

"Thanks, Mama. I thought I should add a little extra something today."

"With your red hair and that green coat, you could be your own festive decoration," Everett teased. "Maybe we should leave you out front to greet everyone who arrives at the party."

"I think not, Papa. I'd freeze to death. Besides, there is no way I'm missing out on all the good food." Gracy gave her father a cheeky smile. "Too bad you'll be so busy as Santa Claus that you likely won't have time to eat."

Everett frowned and turned to his wife. "Tell me that's not true, Cleo. The food at this celebration is something I look forward to all year."

Cleo patted his pillow-stuffed belly. "It shows, dear. It shows."

Gracy couldn't help but laugh as they turned at the corner and joined others heading into the house. Lila and Tom Grove arrived with their little girl and infant son. Nina took one look at Everett and raced over to him, tugging on his hand and chattering so fast, no one, including her parents, could understand her.

"Ho! Ho! Ho!" Everett said, patting her on the head.

Tom swung his daughter into his arms and kissed her rosy cheek. "You can visit with Santa Claus later, Nina. Let's get your brother inside out of the cold."

Lila offered them a friendly smile as she hurried up the steps and inside the house with Tom and their daughter.

"Before you are mobbed by all the children, let's go around to the back door," Gracy suggested, leading the way around the side of the house to the back yard. They'd just started up the steps when the back door swung open and Filly and Ginny stepped out, taking the baskets from them and ushering them inside.

"Oh, the costumes look wonderful! You'll be the stars of the celebration," Filly said, walking in a circle around Everett and Cleo. "The children will be so excited. We were thinking perhaps it would be best to wait until after lunch for you to appear. Would you mind eating here in the kitchen?"

Everett grinned broadly. "In here would be grand. It'll be easier to fill my plate that way."

Cleo playfully swatted his arm. "Santa was just commenting on how much he looks forward to this meal every year."

"I think most of us do," Ginny said, taking their coats from them. "I've been dying to taste a new dessert Alex made, but she and Filly won't let me have even a tiny bite."

"You're worse than Luke with the pumpkin pies," Filly admonished as she motioned to a table pushed back by the windows and out of the way. "You're welcome to settle in. Chauncy is going to ask a blessing on the meal in about five minutes, then perhaps Gracy and I could bring plates to you in here?"

"That sounds lovely, dear," Cleo said, giving Filly an approving nod.

"Help yourself to coffee or tea. There's both sitting there by the stove," Filly said, taking the two lighter baskets they'd brought. "Let's go set out the food, Gracy."

Gracy followed Filly from the kitchen to the dining room. The table fairly groaned from all the food already set out, and the delicious aromas mingling in the air made her mouth water in anticipation of the meal ahead. She'd just set out a platter full of peppermint drop cookies when a shiver of awareness slid from her neck all the way down her spine. She spun around and found herself hauled into Cord's arms.

He gave her a tender hug, then stepped back and offered a sheepish smile. "Hi," he said.

"Hi," she whispered, wondering what had come over him. Maybe he'd been as desperate to see her, to touch her, as she'd been to see him. She lifted a hand and trailed her fingers over his jaw, breathing in the masculine fragrance that was all him.

She drew in a second breath, filling her nose with the appealing scent, then smiled at him. "Happy Christmas Eve."

"And to you, gorgeous Gracy. You look beautiful and festive. I'm quite partial to that outfit." Cord reached out and fingered a fold of velvet in her skirt. "It's as soft as I imagined."

Gracy blushed, vaguely aware that women were rushing around them making final preparations for the meal. She started to take a step away from him, felt herself bumped into from behind, and fell against Cord.

He didn't seem to mind as his arms wrapped around her a second time and he dropped a kiss on her temple. "Thanks, cousin," he said, winking at Lila as she grinned and bustled back toward the kitchen.

"I should go help—" Before she could finish speaking, Bodie raced up to them, his little face animated with excitement.

"Gracy! Gracy! You're here! Guess what? I saw Santa outside! And I got to sleep in Patrick's room last night, and we had bacon for breakfast!"

"All that?" Gracy asked, kneeling and giving Bodie a hug, then settling an arm around him when he pulled back. "It sounds like you've had a big day already."

"Yes! And Daddy said you and the other ladies saved our costumes. I still gets to be a sheep at the program!"

"That's wonderful, Bodie." Gracy offered him an indulgent smile, although she'd completely forgotten about the costumes until that moment. Junie, ever practical, had run back twice to the small room they'd been working in when the fire broke out and retrieved all the costumes. Each of them had grabbed an armful once the door had opened, and they'd carried them across the street to the churchyard before they'd dropped them in the snow and scattered them since a few had been singed by falling embers.

Cord gave her a look full of warmth as someone rang a crystal bell. Although she couldn't see them, Gracy could hear Dora and Merle offer everyone a cheerful welcome to the annual celebration, then Chauncy asked a blessing on the meal and each one gathered there.

"I'm filling plates for Mama and Papa, but I hope you and Bodie will save me a seat to eat with you," Gracy said as people began to enter the dining room to get in the food line.

"You can count on it. Do you need help?"

Gracy shook her head and hurried to step into line. Cord moved in line behind her with Bodie hanging onto his little finger, swinging back and forth from it. "Filly is going to help me. I wouldn't want Bodie to see S-A-N-T-A."

Bodie looked up at her with a frown. "You're spelling words again. I know that means there's a secret."

Gracy tapped the end of his nose and smiled. "It means you'll get a fun surprise after lunch."

His eyes widened. "I will?"

"Definitely." Gracy picked up a plate and began filling it with her father's favorite foods. Filly cut in line in front of her and asked what her mother preferred, then, with a glance back at Cord as he filled a plate for Bodie, Gracy followed Filly to the kitchen.

By the time she returned to the food line, it stretched down the hall. Instead of standing in it, she stepped into the library, where a fire offered cheerful warmth. She moved over to stand in front of it and felt that delicious shiver slide down her spine a second time. A glance over her shoulder confirmed Cord had joined her.

"I thought I saw your skirts swishing this way," he said, taking a step closer to her. "I'm sorry I didn't have a chance to come see you last night. Luke and I were late getting back to his house. I didn't think your folks would appreciate me tapping on the door or your window when it was past midnight."

Gracy shook her head. "That would not have made them, especially Papa, particularly happy. Are you well, Cord? You seemed so unlike yourself yesterday."

"I'm fine, but thank you for asking. How are you? Any lingering cough or other problems?"

"Not really. The cold air made my chest hurt, but I'm sure in a few days I'll be fine."

Suddenly, Gracy felt nervous, like she was waiting for something momentous to happen, although she had no idea what. She glanced around the room, her gaze landing on a kissing ball hanging from the ceiling not a foot from where she and Cord stood. It looked identical to the one Cord had hanging at his home.

She'd avoided getting caught beneath it before, but now she was determined to maneuver Cord so they both stood under it.

With a coy glance at him, she took a step to the right, hoping he'd follow. He not only moved with her but also settled his hand at the curve of her waist.

"You are so lovely, Gracy. So, so lovely and sweet." Cord's voice sounded husky, and his eyes darkened as he edged closer to her.

"Are you familiar with Christmas traditions, Cord?" Gracy asked, tipping her head and grinning at him.

"Most. Why?" He gave her a questioning glance, like she'd lost her mind.

"Do you know the tradition of mistletoe and kissing balls?" She tipped her head back, and his gaze followed hers to the large kissing ball hanging overhead.

Cord smiled a lazy smile and looked at her. "In Tudor times, a kissing bough granted permission for a kiss coming or going, or both. Today, it's a way to steal a kiss from a pretty girl."

"It's not stealing when it's freely given," Gracy said, feeling warm and languid as Cord drew her flush against him and his head lowered to hers.

She'd been thinking about this kiss, dreaming about it, for weeks, but nothing she'd imagined had prepared her for the jolt when their lips connected. The first brush of Cord's lips against hers was tender. The tenderness soon gave way to hunger, then the hunger to passion.

Gracy could have stayed there all day, standing in Cord's loving embrace, experiencing kiss after kiss that left her breathless and tingling from head to toe. This Christmas kiss they exchanged was powerful, potent, and perfect.

Unfortunately, Luke stepped into the room with Blake, and the two men, prone to teasing, made quite a show of clearing their throats and feigning shock at finding Gracy and Cord together.

"I should go check on Mama and Papa," Gracy said, hastily fleeing the room with her face aflame.

On her way out the door, she heard Luke say, "I see you finally figured a few things out, cousin."

She smiled to herself as she returned to the kitchen, then made her way to the dining room to get her father a second helping of several dishes and dessert for both her parents.

When she'd delivered it, she filled a plate for herself and found an empty seat beside Cord at a table where he sat with Lila, Tom, Ginny, and Blake.

Distracted by the kisses she'd shared with Cord and wishing they were still in the library by the fire, she ate without really tasting anything. She'd barely finished the last bite when Luke made an announcement that special visitors were going to arrive any minute and that everyone should go upstairs to the ballroom to greet them.

Gracy slipped out of the room and back to the kitchen, where she adjusted her mother's skirt, fluffed her father's pillow padding, then handed her mother a set of jingle bells to ring. Her father picked up a big red velvet sack that was stuffed with gifts for the children in attendance. Gracy had helped fill bags with nuts and foil-wrapped chocolates. Each child would receive an orange and a small toy as well, but the gifts wouldn't be given until the end of the celebration.

"Ready?" Filly asked as she breezed into the room.

Everett nodded, and Filly led them up a back staircase, then peeked into the hallway and waved at someone.

"Are you ready, children?" Luke asked in a booming voice that carried through the house. "Here comes our special guests!"

Cleo began ringing the bells as she and Everett walked down the hallway to the large ballroom. The children watched, then began excitedly clapping and cheering as Santa and Mrs. Claus arrived. Gracy stood in the doorway, pleased to see Percy Bruner taking photographs.

Bodie was among the smaller children vying for a seat close to Santa. He ended up sitting on one side of Everett while Patrick Granger found a spot on the other. Cleo settled into a tapestry chair in front of the stage and read a Christmas story that had the children enthralled.

After she closed the book, Cleo moved to a seat in the front row of the audience, where the Decker twins scrambled to sit beside her, and Nina Grove climbed up on her lap.

The school-aged children performed a few skits, followed by the annual auction of their craft projects. The top-selling item was a quilt made by three of the older girls, with the help of their mothers.

Alex Guthry, with the assistance of a few of her students, provided a wonderful magic show. At the conclusion, the community band performed several familiar Christmas carols, and on the last one, those gathered for the celebration sang along.

Everett and Cleo moved in front of the stage, where he took a seat in the chair and Cleo handed each child a bag full of goodies after they got a chance to sit with Santa and tell him their wishes.

No one seemed in a hurry to leave, except Cord. He kept glancing outside and then at Gracy. He finally said something to Ginny, who nodded, then he headed straight for Gracy.

"I know this might seem odd, but would you take a little stroll with me?"

Gracy glanced at her parents, who were still deep into the roles of Santa and his wife, then looked at Cord. He seemed anxious and nervous, but she had no idea why. "Of course. I shouldn't be gone long, though. I volunteered to help clean up."

Cord nodded. "I offered to help too. It will only take a minute."

"Let me tell Mama I'll be back shortly." Gracy hurried over to her mother, whispered that she was going outside for a moment but would soon return, then rushed downstairs to find Cord standing in the hallway holding Gracy's green woolen coat. She slid her arms into the sleeves, buttoned it, and walked outside with Cord.

He held his arm out to her, and Gracy took it without hesitation. After his reaction yesterday to her being unharmed, she figured most everyone in town already knew they cared for one another.

Gracy knew without a single doubt she loved Cord, and she always would. She was uncertain of his feelings and his intentions, but she could picture spending the rest of her life with him. What she couldn't envision was a lifetime without Cord and Bodie. She loved them both with all her heart.

"Did you wish to speak about something, Cord, or were you simply in need of fresh air?" Gracy asked as Cord led them not into the heart of town but away from it.

"Both," he said, giving her a sheepish grin. "It's a beautiful Christmas Eve, isn't it?"

Gracy tipped her head back and looked at the blue sky dotted with white clouds. It was a beautiful Christmas Eve, made even more so by the fire having claimed only buildings, but no lives. "It's a wonderful day."

She and Cord walked in silence up a little hill until the town of Hardman was visible below them. It wasn't until Cord stopped, turned to face her, and took her hand in his that she realized he hadn't even worn a coat.

He had on his black cowboy hat and a gun belt, like many of the men in town tended to wear anytime they were out and about. The light blue of his shirt almost matched the sky. Cord Granger was a handsome man by any standard, but Gracy thought what made him most appealing was his caring heart.

Gracy longed, quite desperately, to spend every day—all her days—with Cord.

"Gracy," he said, cupping her elbow with one hand and bringing her hand he held with his other to his lips. He kissed the back of her hand, then each fingertip, turning her knees to butter and scattering her thoughts.

"What is it, Cord?" she asked, about to lose herself in the heat flickering in his eyes.

"I've known it for a while, but yesterday, when I thought I'd lost you, made everything so clear in my mind. I know Christmas, for some, is all about gifts. I've thought about the gift you could give me this year."

"I may have something for you beneath the tree," Gracy said, offering him a teasing smile.

Cord shook his head. "No, that's not what I mean, Gracy. It's the gift of your love that I crave. There's no gift on this earth that could ever compare to that. All I'll ever need is your love, to keep falling deeper and deeper into it each day. Your love is a heavenly treasure, one I vow to never take for granted. I love you, Gracy. I love your spirit and smile, your heart and intelligence. I love the way you cherish my son and adore your parents. I love the way you care about Hardman and doing what you can for the community. You're an amazing, incredible woman, Gracy Randall, and it would be a joy beyond measure if you would consent to marry me and give me the great privilege of being your love. Will you be my bride?"

Gracy gaped at Cord for the length of a heartbeat, then two, before the reality of what he'd just asked sank in.

"Yes! Absolutely yes!" She threw her arms around his neck and he swung her off her feet, holding her tightly to him before he released her just enough to deliver a series of kisses that left her breathless and looking forward to becoming his wife.

"I love you, Gracy!" Cord kissed the tip of her nose and smiled with his heart in his eyes.

"And I love you, Cord. I have since the day we met, even if it took me a while to figure it out. Do you think you'd mind a wedding in January?"

He grinned. "I think that sounds perfect. I'll wire my sister and see if she can make it. You tell me the day, and that's when it will be."

"The second Saturday of January sounds just right," Gracy said, then pulled his head back to hers, giving him a kiss that held hope and promises.

"I love you so, so much, Gracy, and I have a feeling life together won't ever be boring. Sometimes it might be challenging, but together, we can make it through anything."

"I agree," she said, rubbing her hand over the scruff on his face. She wondered if he'd simply forgotten to shave or had plans to grow a beard. Either way, she didn't care. Just as long as he continued to love her, nothing else mattered.

"You truly are the best Christmas gift I could ever ask for, Gracy." He set her on her feet and took a step back. "You look like a Christmas package with that red hair, green coat, and the sprig of holly above your ear. You'll be one package I greatly look forward to unwrapping as soon as we're wed."

Gracy blushed and swatted his arm, making him laugh. "You shouldn't say such things, Mr. Granger."

"I intend to continue to do so as long as they make you blush and smile." Cord took her hand in his and they started back down the hill. "Just so you know, I asked your father for permission to marry you. He and your mother gave their blessing."

Gracy shook her head at him. "Did you really think they'd object? They, along with your Granger cousins, have done everything they could to push us together."

"I am aware of that." Cord smirked. "But they didn't need to work so hard. I've been smitten with you for weeks."

"I just hope you stay smitten for all the years we are wed, Cord."

"Forever, Gracy. Forever."

After they returned to the house, Gracy was too excited to keep the grand news a secret, and soon everyone was abuzz about the upcoming wedding.

That evening, after the church program where Bodie did an excellent job filling the role of a sheep, Cord and Gracy walked back to her parents' house. Bodie had gone ahead with Cleo and Everett, who'd promised to read him a story or two by the fire.

"Soon, my love, you'll be mine." Cord removed her glove and kissed her fingers as they lingered in the porch shadows before going inside the house.

"I'm already yours, Cord. But the wedding will make it official." She smiled and tugged on his hand. "Let's go inside."

Quietly, they stepped into the entry. The heat enveloped them, chasing away the chill as they listened to Cleo reading Bodie a story.

"Just a minute," he whispered, taking a box from his pocket and holding it out to her.

"What is it? Shouldn't I wait until tomorrow to open it?"

"I think you need a little something now," he said, eagerly waiting for her to open the gift.

Gracy untied a red ribbon and tucked it in her coat pocket, then removed the paper and opened the lid on a small box. A beautiful brooch with a gorgeous emerald glittered up at her from a bed of velvet.

"Oh, Cord. It's so lovely," she said, lifting the brooch. He took the box as she unfastened her coat and fastened the brooch to the throat of the emerald silk and ivory lace dress she wore.

"Not nearly as lovely as you, but it will do," he said, grinning at her and kissing her again with a growing fervency.

"Daddy! Are you back?" Bodie called.

"Yep!" Cord pulled away from Gracy, then helped her with her coat. "We're coming, son."

They sat together, drinking hot cider and eating spice cookies as Everett read about Jesus' birth from the Bible, then they sang a few carols before Bodie fell asleep. Cord bundled him up and carried him out to his sleigh with a promise to see Gracy in the morning.

She waved until they were out of sight and returned inside, heart overflowing, as she glanced down at the brooch Cord had given to her. She didn't care about expensive gifts. In fact, if she received nothing this year, it would still be her favorite Christmas because Cord loved her. Truly loved her, and that, to her, seemed like a perfect Christmas miracle.

Chapter Eighteen

Cord straightened his tie, tugged on his sleeves, and nervously smoothed his hair as he stood with Pastor Chauncy Dodd, Luke, and Blake at the front of the church, waiting for Gracy to walk down the aisle and exchange vows with him.

It seemed like ages ago when he'd proposed on Christmas Eve and she'd accepted, even though it had only been two weeks.

Then again, they'd all been so busy in the flurry of the holidays and wedding preparations, the time had sped past.

Today, Gracy would become his wife, and Cord felt like he was getting a second chance at a lifetime of happiness. He knew he and Gracy would continue to argue and banter. Part of him looked forward to it. But he also knew in Gracy he had found a life partner. Someone who wouldn't cower from him or bow to his every wish and whim but a person who shared his dreams and hopes and would stand beside him through whatever came their way.

Yesterday, when he'd stolen a few minutes with Gracy as she'd walked home from Abby Dodd's dress shop, where she'd gone for the final fitting of her wedding dress, they'd spoken of their future. He hadn't been surprised when Gracy had mentioned her hope of giving Bodie brothers and sisters to play with.

Bodie was almost beside himself with excitement. He adored Gracy and was thrilled she was going to be his mother. One of Bodie's favorite things was to go riding with Gracy on his Christmas gift, a pony named Star.

Although Bodie had wanted the pony to be part of the wedding, Gracy had talked Bodie out of it, assuring him Star would not enjoy being in the church or around all the people.

Bodie had reluctantly agreed and was soon distracted by the news he'd get to stay a few nights with Cleo and Everett while Cord and Gracy took a brief honeymoon at home. It was too cold for long journeys, and the nearest train was in Heppner, so they planned to go on a trip to Boston in the spring so Gracy could see where Cord had grown up and he could show her some of his favorite places to visit. Cornelia had already invited them to stay in her home, and Cord looked forward to it.

He glanced at the front pew where his sister and her family sat, and he smiled at her.

Cornelia winked at him, then patted her heart, conveying her joy for him.

The creak of the back door opening signaled Dora Granger Rutherford to begin playing the piano. Cord paid no mind to the two women serving as Gracy's attendants. He had eyes only for his bride as she floated down the aisle in a lace-covered gown of white silk. Her hair was a bright contrast to the pale gown, but she nearly stole his breath from his chest when she smiled at him.

"You be good to my little girl," Everett warned as he placed Gracy's hand in Cord's, then glowered at him.

"I will be, sir."

Everett nodded once, then took a seat by Cleo in the front row opposite of where Cornelia's family sat.

"Dearly beloved, we are gathered here today …" Chauncy spoke, but Cord could hardly pay attention to anything beyond Gracy's beauty. They were halfway through the ceremony before he realized she wore at the neck of her gown the emerald brooch he'd given her for Christmas.

"Do you have the ring?" Chauncy asked, looking from Cord to Luke.

Luke nodded and handed it to Cord, who slipped it onto Gracy's finger as he recited his vows.

Gracy's eyes widened when she realized the ring matched her brooch, then she smiled at Cord with a warmth in her gaze that made him feel overheated.

Somehow, Cord managed to make it through the rest of the ceremony without skipping to the kissing-his-wife part. When Chauncy said he could kiss his bride, Cord took a step closer, but Bodie, who had stood up with him in a new little suit and polished boots, grabbed onto the hem of Cord's suitcoat and tugged.

"What is it, son?" Cord asked, fully distracted by the way Gracy moistened her lips in anticipation of his kiss.

"Kiss her good, Daddy. That's what mommies like. I saw Uncle Luke kissing Aunt Filly, and she—"

Luke settled a hand over Bodie's mouth and pulled him over against his leg, while Filly's face blushed a deep shade of scarlet.

Cord could see the mirth in Gracy's gaze when it melded with his. He slowly bent his head toward hers and gave her a tender kiss. Not one that exuded passion, but a kiss filled with promises.

"Congratulations, Cord and Gracy!" Chauncy proclaimed, and the crowd erupted with cheers.

A reception was held at Dora and Merle's home with most of the town attending.

Cord enjoyed the variety of foods, including a three-layer vanilla cake he was sure Cleo had created because no one except Gracy baked vanilla cakes that tasted like hers.

He'd just finished his second piece when he looked around the room to see Gracy speaking to a friend, her arm around Bodie as he leaned against her, staring up at her like she was the answer to his prayers.

Cord knew Gracy had been the answer to his. He intended to give thanks every single day for the precious gift that was his wife.

A gift he would always treasure even as he remembered their special Christmas kiss.

He hoped they would have many, many Christmases together to share their love and remember the Christmas Eve when he'd proposed and she'd said yes.

"You look like you're one more slap on the back away from bolting, cousin. Why don't you take your bride and leave?" Luke suggested as he moved beside Cord.

"For once, I think you've got a great idea," Cord said, rising from the table where he'd been sitting. He thumped Luke on the back with a grin. "Thanks for everything, Luke. I do appreciate all you and Filly have done since I moved to Hardman."

"That's what family and friends, which I consider you both, are for." Luke smirked at him. "Take that pretty wife of yours and get out of here. I'll ask Alex to do a magic trick or two, and no one will even notice you've gone."

"Perfect."

Cord retrieved his coat and Gracy's from the foyer, then quietly walked up behind his wife, settling the coat over her shoulders. As though she could read his mind, she gave Bodie a kiss on his cheek, whispered something in his ear that sent him scurrying across the room to his cousin Patrick, then winked at Cord and allowed him to lead her down the hall and out the back door.

"I thought you'd never decide to leave," she said as Cord swept her into his arms and carried her out to their waiting sleigh.

Someone had hung paper bells and streamers across the back of it, but Cord didn't care. Not when all that mattered was spending time alone with his magnificent bride.

"You should have let me know you were ready," Cord said, adjusting a heavy throw over Gracy's lap before he climbed into the sleigh. Soon, they were gliding across the snow, heading toward Juniper Creek Ranch. Cord had a few surprises for his bride there, like the cold supper Filly had left for them, and the hothouse roses he'd ordered and placed in several rooms.

"I'm more than ready to embark on the adventure that our life together promises to be," Gracy wrapped her gloved hands around his arm and leaned her head on his shoulder. "I love you so much, Cord, and I'm so, so incredibly thankful to be your wife."

"I'm so grateful and blessed, Gracy, that you allowed me to become your husband. I'll do my best to be a good one and a good father."

"You're already a wonderful father and a good man, Cord. All I need you to do is love me."

"That I can do, my beautiful bride. Just promise me we'll always have Christmas kisses, even in the middle of the summer."

"Always." Gracy offered him a cheeky smile. "I might even keep Maura's kissing ball hanging up all year."

Continue reading for an excerpt from an exciting historical romance that blends heartwarming moments with holiday magic!

Peppermint Drops Recipe

If you are like Cord and love the flavor of peppermint, I hope you'll savor these easy drop cookies. This is an updated version of the cookies he so enjoyed.

Peppermint Drops

½ cup finely crushed peppermint candies (12 candies)
⅔ cup powdered sugar
1 cup butter, softened
1 teaspoon vanilla
½ teaspoon peppermint extract
2 ¼ cups all-purpose flour
¼ teaspoon salt

Preheat oven to 325°F.

Mix ¼ cup crushed candies and ⅓ cup powdered sugar. Set aside.

Mix butter, ⅓ cup powdered sugar, ¼ cup crushed candies, vanilla and peppermint extract in medium bowl. Stir in flour and salt.

Drop dough by tablespoonfuls (or shape into balls) about 2 inches apart on ungreased cookie sheet lined with parchment.

Bake 12 to 13 minutes or until set, but not brown. Immediately remove from cookie sheet; roll in reserved candy mixture.

Cool completely on wire rack. Roll in candy mixture again. Store in air-tight container.

Yield: approximately 3 dozen cookies

Author's Note

I hope you enjoyed another sweet romance in Hardman. I loved writing about Gracy and Cord. When I was thinking about who to include in this book, I thought it would be fun to introduce some new characters as we wait for the next generation of Hardman residents to grow up.

The day I was brainstorming how and where to begin this story, Captain Cavedweller gets the credit for suggesting it be at the ranch with Gracy arriving to find strangers living in her childhood home and a wild child wreaking havoc. I can only imagine what a shock it would be to experience something like that.

The idea for the kissing ball was inspired by one I saw and thought about making last year but ran out of time (no surprise there!). I thought it would be fun for Maura to present it as a decoration to Cord. Since it was a gift from her, he would have felt more compelled to keep it than toss it. Kissing balls have been around a long, long time.

During the Middle Ages, villagers would wind twine and evergreen branches into a ball shape. In the center of the boughs, they would place a clay figure to represent baby Jesus. The boughs were hung from the ceiling to render blessings and good fortune to all who passed beneath it.

It was during Tudor times that the kissing bough became a popular Christmas tradition. They were made with two intertwined hoops covered with evergreens that included holly, bay, and mistletoe, and were hung over doorways to welcome guests. Legend says the tradition of the day was to salute or kiss in greeting or leave-taking. Amid the Christmas season, this bough gave free license for the activity. Those who met beneath it would often pick a berry from the mistletoe as proof of a kiss.

Victorian England brought a new look and name to the ornament. The kissing ball was elaborately decorated, incorporating mistletoe and evergreens such as pine, as well as flowers and herbs. Herbs were chosen for both beauty and symbolic value. Lavender and rosemary signified loyalty and devotion, mistletoe brought good fortune and fertility, while thyme promoted courage. An apple or potato frequently served as the base. Victorians emphasized romance with the kissing ball, waltzing beneath it at parties and women lingering near it in hopes of a suitor catching them there.

I hope Gracy keeps the kissing ball hanging up all year through!

Sometimes Captain Cavedweller amazes me with the unique and thoughtful gifts he gives me. Last year for my birthday, he gave me a collection of promotional booklets from the turn of the century that highlighted everything from popular paint colors for the home to the best products Colgate had to offer. That's where the idea for the soap Gracy so enjoyed, Cashmere Bouquet, came from, as well as Bee Soap. Cashmere Bouquet was introduced in 1872 as the first milled perfumed soap. It was viewed more as a luxury item for many years. It was produced for more than 130 years by the

Colgate company. If you want to smell it for yourself, you can still find bars of it on sites like eBay.

In the story, when Filly mentions Patrick and Bodie trying to beat off a cast with a hammer, the inspiration for that tidbit came from something my dad and his cousin did when they were rascally boys. From the stories I've heard, Dad and Willie were often in cahoots in some type of shenanigan that landed them in trouble with my grandmother or great-aunt.

When I was browsing through the December 1909 issues of the Heppner Gazette for news that might inspire some dialogue for my characters, I happened upon a column of "brief news of the past week." They certainly meant brief when they stated it. The column included a bunch of one-line "articles." The one that caught my eye, though, was, "A woman is walking from Shoshone to Denver on a wager." Wait, what? I had so many questions. An online search didn't turn up any immediate answers, although I did happen across several articles about Edward Payson Weston and mentioned him in the story. If you have any detail about the woman who made that walk, I'd love to learn more!

As for Edward Payson Weston, he was quite well known in his day for his publicized walks. He really did embark on a cross-country trip that began in New York on his seventieth birthday in 1909.

Snickerdoodles are one of Captain Cavedweller's favorite cookies. I've included them in a few other stories as a nod to him, but I thought it would be fun for them to be Bodie's favorite cookie. From what I could discover, the first appearance of them in a recipe book was in 1902.

Mup is the name of Bodie's toy horse. It's an odd name, but that's an acknowledgement of my little nephew. When he was barely talking, his parents got a cat, and he named it Mup. No one knows why, but it's a fun name to say!

Thank you again for reading another adventure in Hardman. Who do you think should be included in a future story?

Special thanks to Allison, Alice, Linda, and my Hopeless Romantics team for their help in making this book the best it can be!

Wishing you and your loved ones a glorious holiday season!

All my best,
Shanna

Thank You!

Thank you for reading Gracy and Cord's story. If you enjoyed *The Christmas Kiss*, please consider writing a review? I would be so grateful to you if you did.

If you haven't yet, subscribe to my newsletter. You'll receive a free book or two, and what I call *The Welcome Letters* with exclusive content and some fun stuff! My newsletters are sent when I have new releases, sales, or news of freebies to share. Each month, you can enter a contest, get a new recipe to try, and discover details about upcoming events. Don't wait. Sign up today!

Make sure you don't miss any books in the *Hardman Holidays* series!

Preview of Holiday Hope

Holiday Express
Four generations discover the wonder of the
season and the magic of one very special train
in these sweet holiday romances.

Begin the journey with *Holiday Hope*

1884

A bump in the track jostled Cora Lee Schuster
from a restless slumber. Weary from days of travel
across the great expanse of the United States, she
hesitated to open her eyes and begin the day.

She'd climbed into the upper berth of the train
car more than ready to rest last night, but sleep had
proven elusive through the long midnight hours.

Plagued by thoughts of what her immediate
future might hold when she arrived in Holiday, a
newly constructed town in the wilds of Eastern
Oregon, she found it impossible to relax and fully
surrender to her dreams.

Had she been completely crazy to travel all the
way from Cincinnati to marry a rancher? She
supposed the answer to that question would become

clear soon enough. By noon, the train would arrive in Holiday and she'd meet her intended, Jude Coleman. Would he be a man as gritty and tough as the images his name conjured in her mind? Or someone kind? Someone she could come to love?

Cora Lee drew in a deep breath, needing to clear her thoughts. Instead of a cleansing lungful of air, she inhaled a stale, sour odor that put her in mind of rancid cabbage. Nose wrinkled in disgust, she started to rise, only to find the braid she'd fashioned last night pinned down, prohibiting any movement.

Curious, she reached up and felt around the top of her pillow until her fingers encountered something both bony and hairy. A scream clawed upward in her throat as she envisioned a wild animal curled around her head. When the offending weight shifted, she squelched the urge to shriek and quickly sat up. She glanced over her shoulder to see two incredibly large, hairy feet resting in her berth.

Cora Lee rolled her eyes, then glanced down at a noise from the berth below her. Anne Charles, her newly acquainted friend, pressed a hand over her mouth to keep from bursting into laughter. When Cora Lee made a silly face, the two women could no longer hold back their humor. Cora Lee buried her face into the mattress while Anne held a pillow over her face.

Once their amusement subsided, Anne rolled to the edge of her berth and shook her head. "What a way to begin your day," she whispered.

"I thought something had crawled by my head and died," Cora Lee spoke in a hushed tone.

"Maybe the fellow has passed on to glory and that's why his feet stink so much."

"Shh! He might hear you. At least, I hope that those gigantic things belong to a man. I'd hate to think of a woman having such enormous feet or hairy legs!"

Just then, the feet twitched, and the owner pulled them back inside his berth, causing the two women to laugh again.

"We might as well get ready for the day," Anne said, reaching beneath her berth and handing Cora Lee her satchel.

"Agreed. If we hurry, we might even beat the line to the lavatory," Cora Lee said, hurrying to dress in the cramped quarters. Hastily changing from her nightgown into a traveling dress that would forever be embedded with soot from the coal that powered the train down the track, she sat cross-legged on the bed, combing her hair, her mouth full of hairpins. The train lurched around a curve, throwing her off balance. She spewed the hairpins onto her lap, lest she swallow them. Grasping onto the berth brace kept her from shooting right off the bed, but her traveling companion didn't fare as well.

Anne squealed as she was thrown out of her berth into the center aisle, landing on her backside with her dress slipping down one shoulder.

Cora Lee shoved the pins into her hair, hopped off the berth, and stepped between Anne and two interested-appearing men dressed in western garb as they moved closer. She held a hand out to Anne, helped her to her feet, then pushed her back behind the curtain surrounding their berth. With a curt nod to the men, she followed Anne into the bit of privacy afforded by the curtain and helped to right the woman's rumpled clothing.

"Well, that's one way to get the blood flowing first thing," Cora Lee said with a smile.

"I am mortified!" Anne hissed. Her entire face was a bright shade of pink as she smoothed her dress, then nervously fussed with her hair.

"Don't be. At least you didn't have smelly feet next to your face."

Anne's tense shoulders relaxed slightly. "True. I only fell into the midst of the car with men ogling me from every direction," she said with a hint of sarcasm.

"Oh, it wasn't nearly that dramatic." Cora Lee took the brush from Anne and gave the woman's luxuriant brown hair several strokes before fashioning it into the high pompadour her friend favored. "There. All ready."

"Perhaps those who were awake returned to sleep," Anne said as they pulled back the curtains and stepped into the aisle.

"Or it could be everyone was awakened by our jolting ride," Cora Lee said, leading the way to the lavatory. At least they were fortunate to be traveling in a car that had a lavatory for ladies and another for gentlemen. In fact, Cora Lee had been both surprised and amazed by how nice her accommodations had been the entire trip. She'd half-anticipated traveling in the immigrant car, but for the most part, she'd been comfortable and well-fed.

As she and Anne waited for a turn in the lavatory, she glanced at the woman with whom she'd felt an immediate kinship. They'd met in Omaha while they were waiting to board the train that would carry them west. Anne was a proper Englishwoman. She'd arrived in America a year ago with her maidenly aunt. The woman had passed not long after they'd settled into a small home in New York City. It had taken Anne months to sort through the paperwork, only to discover the woman who was also her guardian had left her penniless. Unable to find suitable work, Anne had decided to take a chance on the unknown and become a mail-order bride.

Cora Lee could well relate to Anne and her story of being forced to make a choice between poverty, working in a deplorable job, or accepting an offer of marriage from a complete stranger. The idea of marriage seemed far more palatable than the other options, so here she was on her way to Holiday.

The discovery that Holiday was also Anne's destination nearly made her weep with joy. Anne had agreed to wed the owner of the local livery and blacksmith shop. Cora Lee could hardly envision the petite, elegant Anne married to some hulking brute who smelled of sweat, iron, and horses, but she hoped her friend would find happiness in the unconventional union.

Cora Lee contemplated her own impending marriage to a man she didn't know. The last letter she'd received from Jude had said he'd give her time to get acclimated to ranch life before they wed.

At least she wouldn't be immediately pressed into the role of a wife.

She knew from Jude's letters that he resided on Elk Creek Ranch, just north of town. He, along with his father and brother, raised beef cattle and also trained horses they sold to the military. Jude had also mentioned their property included timber, so she assumed the town had to be in the mountains or close to them.

She'd never heard of Holiday before she'd answered Jude's advertisement for a wife. She'd even attempted to locate the town on a map, but it had only been founded six years prior when a large gold strike drew men to the area. Now that money poured into town from the mine, respectable businesses had been established and many men actively sought wives.

Cora Lee had spent her entire life residing in a busy city. Her family had never even owned a horse, or a dog, living in an apartment above her father's shoe store. Oh, they'd been happy, the three of them. Her father had provided well for his family by making and repairing shoes, and her mother had created a wonderful, loving home for them all to enjoy.

Now her parents were gone, and Cora Lee had been left without many options for her future.

The closer she got to Holiday, the more she questioned if she'd chosen the right path. What if her intended was a horrible man, one who'd written lies to her? She'd heard about mail-order brides being deceived. There hadn't been time to exchange photographs with Jude, even if she'd had a recent one to send, which she did not.

No, the last photo that had been taken of her was carefully packed in her trunks with other keepsakes that would remind her of her parents and her heritage.

"I shall greatly look forward to our arrival in Holiday, if for no other reason than to conclude our time being tossed about on a rocking, rumbling train," Anne said as they finished in the lavatory and returned to their seats. The porter had folded up the berths, pushed aside the curtains, and made the area ready for the day.

Cora Lee nodded. "It will be nice to have this long journey behind us." She stowed her satchel beneath the seat, pinned on her hat, and settled back as the train continued chugging down the tracks.

Anne and Cora Lee purchased breakfast when the train stopped at a small town just across the Idaho border in Oregon. A farmer and his wife boarded, selling fresh milk, hot doughnuts, and boiled eggs. The two women gladly parted with a few coins for the food and enjoyed every bite as the train pulled away from the station.

Two hours later, the porter walked through the passenger car. "Baker City, folks. Baker City coming right up."

"Pardon me, sir," Anne said, smiling up at the man. "Might you be able to confirm the travel arrangements for the remainder of our journey?" She handed him her ticket.

"Yes, ma'am," he said with a friendly smile. "You'll switch trains in Baker City. The Holiday

Express line will take you right into Holiday. You can't miss it. That train is a beaut, shiny like a new penny." He tipped his cap to them, returned the ticket to Anne, and continued on his way through the car and on to the next one.

"I wish we had time to explore Baker City," Anne said, looking out the window as the train rolled past a sea of cattle. Cowboys rode along a fence, and one of them lifted his hat, offering a jaunty wave.

"I wonder if all the men here are like that," Cora Lee asked as she gazed out the window, fighting down the urge to return the welcoming greeting.

She'd expected the landscape to be different, but nothing had prepared her for the rolling hills covered in what she'd learned was called sagebrush. It seemed almost barren, desolate, to her, although not quite as lonesome as the prairies they'd traveled across. Would Holiday be surrounded by scrubby brush, dirt, and not much else? She hoped not.

Although it was just the first day of November, she'd expected to see snow on the ground, but it appeared none had yet fallen. That, at least, made traveling easier for everyone.

She and Anne were both watching out the window as the train rolled into the station at Baker City. True to what they'd heard about the mining town, it was bustling with activity.

"Welcome to Baker City," the porter said as he took a position at the steps leading out of the car to help the women as they departed the train.

"Perhaps another time, we can travel back here to investigate what appears to be a thriving town," Anne said as they made their way over to where a train, as shiny and new as the porter said, was loading passengers. It didn't hold any sleeping cars, but the passenger car they stepped into was nicely appointed, with upholstered seats all facing forward.

"How lovely," Anne said, smoothing her gloved hand over the back of a seat. "Would you like to sit by the window or the aisle?"

"The aisle's fine with me," Cora Lee said, settling beside her friend. They slid their satchels beneath the seats, sank back against the soft cushions, and anxiously awaited the beginning of the last leg of their journey. Cora Lee took in the mahogany paneling, the stained glass framing the windows, the extraordinary details of the passenger car that made her feel like she'd entered a luxurious world she'd only dreamed of one day experiencing.

They didn't have long to wait before the train began to move and chugged away from the station. From what Cora Lee could tell, they were heading due east, but she knew from Jude's letters that Holiday was located north of Baker City.

Curious, but not concerned, she and Anne stared out the window at the hills of sagebrush.

"This must seem even stranger to you than it does to me," she said to her seatmate.

Anne turned to smile at her. "Oh, I think it is probably quite different than either of us anticipated, but perhaps there is beauty to be found in the ruggedness of this place."

"It is rather rugged," Cora Lee said, patting Anne's hand as they returned to watching out the window.

"Did you notice the name painted on the engine of the train?"

"Hope." Cora Lee thought the name of the train quite fitting. Earnestly, she hoped she'd done the right thing in agreeing to come to Holiday to marry a stranger. "I can't think of a better name for the conveyance carrying us to the end of our journey. Hope is what I have for our future, and hope is what we'll have to lean on as we begin a new life in Holiday."

"Exactly. We shall cling to hope and friendship and faith." Anne playfully bumped her arm. "And perhaps our handsome husbands."

Cora Lee laughed. "I *hope* it will be so."

As the train chugged down the tracks, it changed directions, traveling north. With each passing mile, Cora Lee grew more nervous until she felt like she might explode. What if this trip had been a huge mistake? What if Jude was a horrid man? What if she spent the rest of her life in misery?

Unable to sit still, she rose from her seat.

"Where are you going?" Anne asked, glancing from the window to Cora Lee. "Is something wrong?"

"I just need to stretch my legs a bit."

Anne nodded in commiseration. "I can hardly wait to go for a stroll through Holiday. It will be nice to walk after sitting for so many days on end." The woman rose slightly and glanced toward the back of the car. "Perhaps no one would mind if you walk from one end of the car to the other a few times."

"I guess we'll find out," Cora Lee said, taking a few steps to the front of the car. She turned, then headed toward the back. She'd nearly reached the door when the train jerked, brakes squealing, and a few passengers shouted in surprise as they ground to an unexpected, bone-jarring halt.

She cast a questioning look over her shoulder toward Anne. What on earth was happening?

Available now on Amazon!

About the Author

PHOTO BY SHANA BAILEY PHOTOGRAPHY

USA Today bestselling author Shanna Hatfield is a farm girl who loves to write. Her sweet historical and contemporary romances are filled with sarcasm, humor, hope, and hunky heroes.

When Shanna isn't dreaming up unforgettable characters, twisting plots, or covertly seeking dark, decadent chocolate, she hangs out with her beloved husband, Captain Cavedweller, at their home in the Pacific Northwest.

Shanna loves to hear from readers.
Connect with her online:
Website: shannahatfield.com
Email: shanna@shannahatfield.com

Printed in Great Britain
by Amazon

31784622R00165